RUSTIC CARPENTRY
WOODWORKING WITH NATURAL TIMBER

EDITED BY PAUL N. HASLUCK
INTRODUCTION BY RALPH KYLLOE

SKYHORSE PUBLISHING

Skyhorse Publishing books may be purchased in bulk at special discounts for sales promotion, corporate gifts, fund-raising, or educational purposes. Special editions can also be created to specifications. For details, contact the Special Sales Department, Skyhorse Publishing, 307 West 36th Street, 11th Floor, New York, NY 10018 or info@skyhorsepublishing.com.

Skyhorse® and Skyhorse Publishing® are registered trademarks of Skyhorse Publishing, Inc.®, a Delaware corporation.

Visit our website at www.skyhorsepublishing.com.

10 9 8 7 6 5 4 3

Library of Congress Cataloging-in-Publication Data

Rustic carpentry : woodworking with natural timber / edited by Paul N. Hasluck ; introduction by Ralph Kylloe.
    p. cm.
"Originally published 1907 by Cassell and Company, Ltd."
Includes bibliographical references and index.
ISBN-13: 978-1-60239-121-5 (pbk. : alk. paper)
ISBN-10: 1-60239-121-1 (pbk. : alk. paper)
1. Rustic woodwork. I. Hasluck, Paul N. (Paul Nooncree), 1854-1931

TT200.R79 2007
684'.08—dc22
                              2007013051

Printed in the United States of America

CONTENTS

INTRODUCTION BY RALPH KYLLOE

One day, long ago, a Caveman rolled a log over in front of a fire pit and sat down. That log was the first piece of furniture! Rustic in every way, the log no doubt retained all of its original burls, twists, contortions, and probably a few branches and some bark as well. It was a great invention! The materials were there for the choosing. Big people could have big logs and little people could use little logs as seating. It's safe to guess that shortly after the invention of the log chair some brilliant guy put a few branches together and created the first table!

Then iron was invented. Once hard metal became available, people created all kinds of saws, files, hammers, and nails. And just a few hundred years after that we had Lazy Boy recliners! With the industrial revolution came things that didn't look at all like the organic materials they were created from. Through all this, our lives have become more complex than our ancestors could have imagined. We sit in high-tech desk chairs staring at computer screens, watch television from plush synthetic sofas, and live in homes made of materials we don't understand. Yet every once in a while nature pokes us in the ribs, begging our attention. To appease her, we fill our homes with plants and pets, vacation in the great outdoors, and dabble in rustic furniture!

The back-to-nature movement is not new. Every major philosopher throughout history has argued for a simpler life. Thoreau and many others wrote volumes about the joys of nature. The Romantics argued for a deepened appreciation of all things natural and for the creative spirit inherent in all humanity. Today, because of our deepening involvement in technology and our disassociation with the environment, our collected common sense invites us to return to something that we can comprehend, something we can feel and touch.

Throughout all of humanity the drive to create exists. As a species we've invented all sorts of things, each designed, in some way, to make our lives a bit easier or more beautiful. In many respects, we're a very sophisticated species. Our brains require us to expand on the simple and to keep active. In education we refer to this phenomenon as the "Theory of Maximum Arousal." Some people make quilts, whirligigs, or toys, others create gardens, or paint paintings. And some people make rustic furniture.

Rustic furniture is unique. It's full of humor and folly. It is not taken seriously. It is also, however, full of attitude and abandon. It's almost a slap in the face to high technology and high society. It's replete with charm and personality. And all of the twists, turns, and aberrations inherent in the materials used make it more inviting. There is little or no attempt to alter or disguise the materials used in rustic furniture. It's real and honest stuff—the more organic the better.

Rustic furniture is not solely the creation of Americans. Every society throughout the world has some form of it. Early wood block prints from China show images of wildly organic tables, chairs, and settees made from roots and branches. Rustic furniture has been found in Italy, throughout Scandinavia, Russia, and South America. This has been going on for thousands of generations—the earliest accounts of rustic furniture and log cabins date to about ten thousand years ago!

In truth, the building of rustic furniture has changed little over the years. To make the simplest furniture all you really need is a saw, hammer, nails, and a few other tools; the bigger pieces of furniture don't require much more! Even though *Rustic Carpentry* was first written in 1907, the information contained in this book is all that's necessary to start creating rustic furniture. Equally important is the artwork on these pages, which offer a rare glimpse into the aesthetic of the day. Ideas of balance, form, and scale—all the elements of beauty and perception—are really no different today than when the pieces shown were created a century ago.

Rustic furniture is a passion I've enjoyed for more than thirty years. A classic folk art, rustic furniture done well can thrill viewers and shape cultures. This book is a perfect place to start.

LIST OF ILLUSTRATIONS

RUSTIC CARPENTRY

—◆◇◆—

CHAPTER I.

LIGHT RUSTIC WORK.

RUSTIC carpentry does not demand great skill in woodworking, but it does require a large amount of artistic perception. The tools needed are but few, and the materials employed are comparatively cheap, although in many districts they are becoming dearer every year.

It may be said that any articles made from the now popular bamboo may be made quite as effectively in light rustic work.

For light rustic work, sticks of hazel, cherry, yew, blackthorn, birch, larch, fir, and the prunings of many varieties of shrubs may be used; but it is necessary that the material should be cut at the proper season, and thoroughly dried before being worked up. The sticks should be cut in mid-winter, as at that time the sap is at rest; if cut in the summer time the bark will peel off. If peeled sticks are required, they should be cut in the spring, when the sap is rising, as at that time the rind will come off easily. In some districts the copses are cleared of undergrowth periodically, and the sticks (generally hazel) sold to hurdle and spar makers. A selection of these sticks would be very suitable for the purpose here described.

The sticks should be stacked in an open shed in an upright position if possible, and in such a manner that the air can freely circulate around them. When they are required for fishing rods or walking sticks they are hung up to season— this keeps them straighter; but the hanging of them up is not necessary for the work about to be dealt with. When the sticks have been put away for from six to twelve months, according to size,

Fig. 1.—Photograph Frame and Wall Bracket Combined.

they will be ready for use, after being rubbed with a cloth or brushed to clean off the dust and bring up the colour of the bark. Fir cones may often be worked into a design, and bits of rough bark and the warts and burrs found on old elm trees may be collected by the rustic worker and put by for future use.

One method of treatment for designs in light rustic work is to split the sticks and use them to overlay the work with a Swiss pattern, as shown by Fig. 1; another method is to work the sticks up after the manner that canes are used in bamboo furniture (see Figs. 3 and 42, pp. 12 and 36).

Fig. 1 represents a wall bracket with a photograph or mirror in the frame. To make this, the piece forming the back is first cut out of $\frac{3}{8}$-in. deal. The shelf, of $\frac{3}{4}$-in. deal, is then nailed to

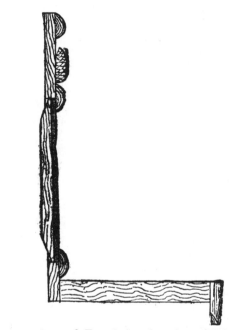

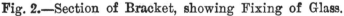

Fig. 2.—Section of Bracket, showing Fixing of Glass.

the bottom edge. Some straight hazel, fir, or other sticks are next selected and split; these are nailed round the edges of the back, and round the opening at the centre. The pieces round the opening overlap the edges about $\frac{1}{4}$ in., to form a rebate for the glass. The bare spaces at the sides and top may be covered in the following manner : Take a piece of brown elm bark and run a saw into it. Catch the sawdust, and, after warming the wood, cover it with thin glue. Sprinkle the

brown sawdust on the glued surface, and sufficient will adhere to cover the deal and give the
frame a rustic appearance. Cork-dust or filings
may be used instead of sawdust. Bunches of fir

Fig. 3.—Small Easel in Rustic Work.

or larch cones are nailed to the corners, as illustrated; these should be pared at the back with
knife or chisel to a flat surface. The outer edge
of the shelf is finished with an edging of short

lengths of split stick nailed on. The general construction of the bracket, and the method of fixing the glass, will be clear from Fig. 2, which is a section through the centre.

A small easel for photographs, or, if constructed larger, for a fire-screen, is shown by Fig. 3. It is made entirely of round sticks. Fig. 4 illustrates the method of attaching the back support—namely, by means of a couple of staples, which may be made out of a hairpin. In jointing round sticks together, the joints may be mitred by notching a V-shaped piece out of

Fig. 4.—Method of Attach-   Fig. 5.—Mitred Joint.
ing Support to Easel.

one stick and cutting the other to fit (Fig. 5); or a mortise and tenon, as represented by Fig. 6, may be used.

In making the easel (Fig. 3), the top and bottom bars are mitred to the sides, and the central upright to the top and bottom bars. The joints are secured by either brads or panel pins. Care must be taken to bore for the nails with a bradawl, as nothing looks worse than splits in the work. The upright piece in the centre of the top bar may be secured by driving a long panel pin into the lower upright through the top bar, filing the head to a point to form a dowel, and driving the top piece on with a hammer. Where a small stick is joined to a larger one, as in the case of the filling-in pieces, a flat may be made with a knife or chisel on the larger stick, and the smaller one cut to fit and nailed on.   In making a small easel, only a single stick attached to the

Fig. 6.—Mortise and Tenon Joint

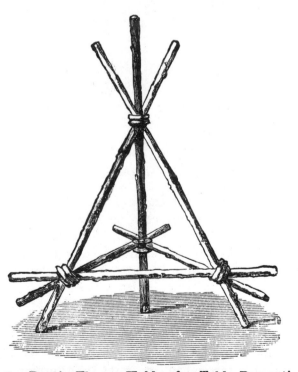

Fig. 7.—Rustic Flower Holder for Table Decoration.

centre upright will be required to form a back support, but for a larger one it will be preferable to frame it as shown by Fig. 3.

The finished articles may be either stained and varnished or left plain. Cherry sticks look well if the bark is left the natural colour, and the ends, where exposed, cleaned off and varnished

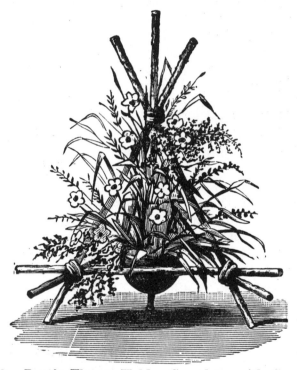

Fig. 8.—Rustic Flower Holder Complete, with Cocoanut Vase in Position.

without being stained. Some sticks improve in colour if rubbed over with a rag moistened with linseed oil.

If a stain is required, one that is sold in bottles would be suitable, but a little vandyke brown, ground in water, and applied with a sponge, answers the purpose. Sometimes, as in the case of the table top (see Fig. 42, p. 36), it is

a good plan to stain the wood before nailing on
the pattern work, or there will be danger, if the
sticks are dark in colour, of the lighter wood
showing through.

If the rustic work is intended to be placed
out of doors, it should be given two or three
coats of hard outside varnish.

The rustic flower-holder for table decoration,
shown by Fig. 7, consists simply of a gipsy tripod
formed with six rustic sticks, put together in th
form shown, and tied with a length of bass.
There is no attempt made at finish, but the sticks
must be firmly tied together at the joints, and
the ends of the bass can be left either hanging
loose or tied in a bow. The holder for the flowers
is a cocoanut shell, which has been sawn in two,
so as to leave one part a sort of cup or egg
shape; three holes are bored with a bradawl at
equal distances round the edge, and it is suspended from the tripod with three more pieces of
the bass, which completes the arrangement. Of
course, any small receptacle can be used in place
of the cocoanut shell, but that, perhaps, carries
out the rustic appearance the best, and is very
easily obtained. Fig. 8 is an attempt to show the
tripod when decorated.

The rustic hall-stand shown by Figs. 9 to 11
was made actually from branches and twigs of an
old apple tree. The uprights and principal cross-
pieces are $\frac{7}{8}$ in. thick, and the criss-cross pieces
are $\frac{1}{2}$ in. thick. The bottom is made of four pieces
$1\frac{1}{2}$ in. thick. The longer ones measure 1 ft. 8 in.,
and the shorter ones 1 ft. 2 in.; they are nailed
together in such a manner that the ends at the
two front corners each cross and project $2\frac{1}{2}$ in.
The front uprights are 2 ft. high, the back ones
2 ft. 2 in.; the longer cross-pieces are 1 ft. 8 in.,
the shorter 11 in. The ends intersect and project
3 in. at each of the front corners; only the long-
est piece projects 3 in. at the back corners, the

shorter pieces being cut off flush with the frame
to allow of the stand fitting close to a wall. These
cross-pieces are nailed to the uprights to allow

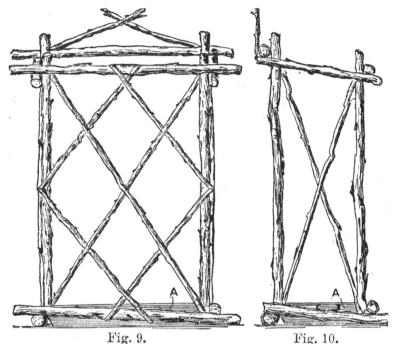

Fig. 9.   Fig. 10.

Figs. 9 and 10.—Front and Side Elevations of Rustic
Hall Stand

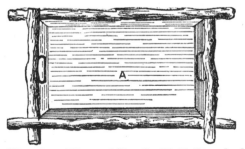

Fig. 11.—Plan of Rustic Hall Stand, showing Umbrella Pan.

the top ends of the latter to project 2 in. above
them, this bringing the measurement of the ob-
long inner framework to 1 ft. 10 in. by 1 ft. 2 in.

The thin pieces are nailed on as shown in Fig. 9,
being interlaced as much as possible. The back of
the stand is treated in a similar manner. The
whole of the wood is used as rough as possible,
the bark being retained, with the knots, etc. ; the
ends are, however, pared off smooth with a chisel.
Two coats of varnish finish the stand, save for the
addition of a receptacle to catch the drainings

Fig. 12.

Fig. 13.

Figs. 12 and 13.—Elevation and Plan of Plant Stool.

from umbrellas, and for this the stand illustrated
has a painted baking-tin A (Fig. 11).

The rustic stool (Figs. 12 and 13) is intended
to be made in pairs, and placed one on each side
of the umbrella-stand above described, each supporting a plant, such as a fern or palm. The
top of each stool is cut from 9 in. square 1-in.
wood (wood from an old box answers well), and
is sawn into an octagonal shape. A double row
of pieces of apple, maple, or some other wood
with good bark, is nailed around the edges,
thicker pieces being used at the bottom than at

the top to give a graduated appearance. The entire top is then covered with straight pieces of stick, selected for the beauty of their bark. All pieces are nailed on with cut brads. The four legs are formed of 1-in. apple-wood 9 in. long. They are bevelled at the top to fit a square block of wood, 2 in. thick and 3 in. long, which is firmly secured to the top by two screws. This piece of wood should be fastened to the top before the rustic rods are placed in position. Two $2\frac{1}{2}$-in. wire nails through each of the legs hold them quite securely to the central block. Portions of rustic wood, from $\frac{1}{4}$ in. to $\frac{3}{8}$ in. in diameter, are

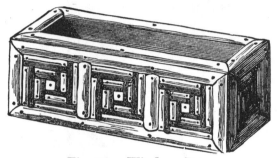

Fig. 14.—Window Box.

then nailed across the legs, as shown in Fig. 12, the ends being allowed to cross each other and project about 1 in. all ways. The whole stool, when finished, stands $10\frac{1}{2}$ in. high, and is so strong that it will support a heavy man with safety. The block of wood to which the legs are attached should be stained to match the rustic wood; permanganate of potash solution will effect this. Finally, two coats of clear varnish give a good finish to the work.

Window boxes are illustrated by Figs. 14 to 16. That shown by Fig. 14 is made from a raisin box obtained from a grocer. Such boxes are not costly, and to buy and knock these up for rough uses is often more economical than buying new

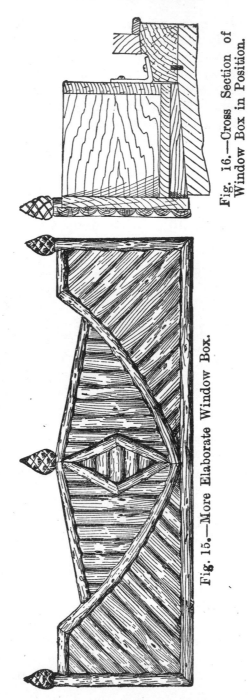

Fig. 16.—Cross Section of Window Box in Position.

Fig. 15.—More Elaborate Window Box.

material. Take care that the boards are stout enough to hold the brads firmly. The box measures about 21 in. by 7 in. by 7 in., and is wholly covered with mosaic of dark and light strips in panels. Strips are also nailed on the upper edges.

The more elaborate window box (Figs. 15 and 16) can be made of a size to fit the window for which it is intended. A few holes should be bored in the bottom for drainage, and the front board is cut to the shape shown and the rustic ornament is nailed to the box and forms no part of the construction. In Fig. 16 wedge pieces are shown fitted to the stone sill to bring the box level; it is kept in position by two metal angle-pieces screwed both to the wood sill and to the back of the box.

CHAPTER II.

FLOWER STANDS, VASES, ETC.

THE rustic-work flower stand (Fig. 17) may be 3 ft. high by 3 ft. 6 in. long by 9 in. wide. For the legs, select four curved saplings 3 ft. 3 in. long by 2½ in. in diameter; and as some difficulty may be experienced in obtaining them with the natural curves sufficiently alike, artificial methods of bending must be resorted to. Therefore get the saplings from 2 ft. to 3 ft. longer than the finished length, and bend them to shape by means of the Spanish windlass as shown in Fig. 18. Flexible six-strand fixing wire or stout hemp cord can be used; or a straining screw and link, as employed for tightening fencing wire, will answer equally well; keep the tension on till the wood is curved permanently, the time varying with the nature and condition of the wood, and the strain being applied gradually at intervals. The rails are tenoned to fit mortises in the legs, and battens are nailed to the lower long rails, to support the flower pots (see Fig. 19). The rustic work is then fixed diagonally to the rails. The ends that abut against the legs and centre-piece are pared away so as to make a neat joint, and angle boards are fitted to the under side of the lower rails to support the rustic work where it curves downwards.

The vase shown by Fig. 20 is hexagonal in shape, with vandyked sides fixed to a base supported upon tripod legs, and stands about 3 ft. 3 in. high. Elm boards are suitable for the sides and bottom; they are 1 ft. 3 in. high by 9 in. wide at the top end, and 6½ in. wide at the bottom by 1 in. thick. Shoot the edges of the

boards to a bevel of 60°, and fix them with nails
driven as shown at Fig. 21. When the six sides
are completed, prepare the hexagon baseboard to
suit. Bore holes in it for drainage, and also bore

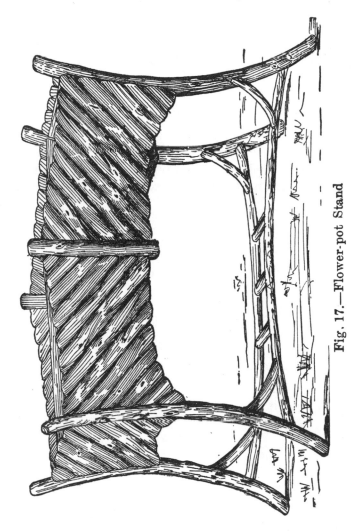

Fig. 17.—Flower-pot Stand

three equidistant holes, $1\frac{1}{4}$ in. in diameter, at an
angle of about 60°, for the tenons of the legs to
enter (see Fig. 22). Next screw the base to the
sides, and fix on the barked rustic work. The

twigs for this should be seasoned at least one year before using. They are sawn in halves, straight twigs being selected for the purpose. If

Fig. 18.—Method of Bending Saplings.

necessary, shoot the edges slightly, so as to obtain a closer fit when fixing them in parallel. Begin by attaching the lower border to the hexagonal base, then the upright pieces over the angles, hollowed

Fig. 19.—Fixing Rails, etc., to Posts.

as shown at Fig. 23; next fix the top sloping pieces, and finally the horizontal twigs. The legs are nailed at the base of the vase (see Fig. 22);

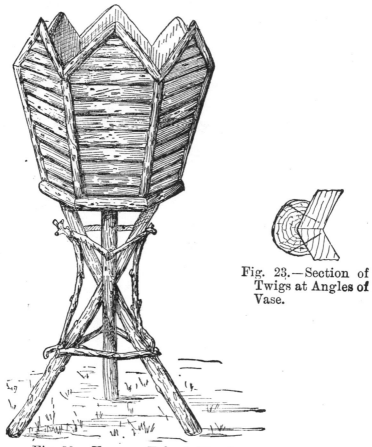

Fig. 20.—Vase on Tripod Stand.

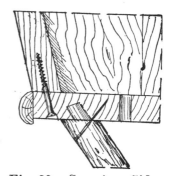

Fig. 23.—Section of Twigs at Angles of Vase.

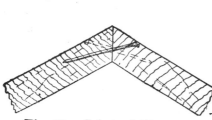

Fig. 21.—Joint of Hexagon Sides of Vase.

Fig. 22.—Securing Sides and Legs of Vase to Base.

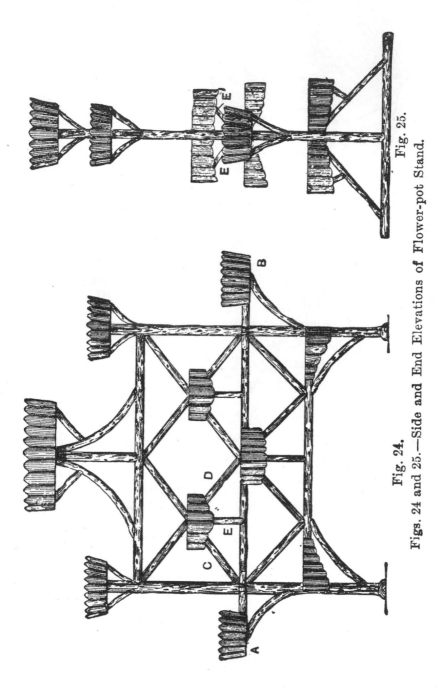

Fig. 25.

Fig. 24.

Figs. 24 and 25.—Side and End Elevations of Flower-pot Stand.

and at the centre, where they cross, they are
further secured with twigs, which do the duty of
rungs, as shown in Fig. 20.

The flower stand shown in front and end view

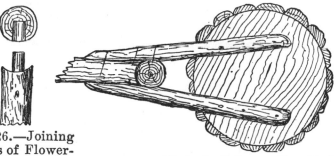

Fig. 26.—Joining
Rails of Flower-
pot Stand to Up-
rights.

Fig. 27.—Method of Supporting End
Shelves of Flower-pot Stand at A
and B (Fig. 24).

by Figs. 24 and 25 has accommodation for sixteen
pots. The two uprights are 2 ft. 8 in. high by
about 2½ in. in diameter. The three rails are
2 ft. 9 in. long, and are tenoned to the posts as
shown by Fig. 26; the posts are also tenoned and
nailed to the sills (bottom rails), and strutted, as
shown in Fig. 25. The method of fixing the
shelves A and B (Fig. 24) is shown in Fig. 27,
which is an under-side view; struts are also fitted,
as shown in Fig. 25. The method of fixing the

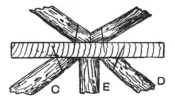

Fig. 28.—Fixing Centre Shelves of Flower-pot Stand.

centre shelves is indicated at Fig. 28. The shelf,
and also the struts C, D, E, and E[1] (Figs. 24 and
25), are fixed to the centre rail; then the top
diagonal braces are nailed to both the shelf and

the top rail, thus keeping the whole secure. The
remainder of the work calls for no special in-

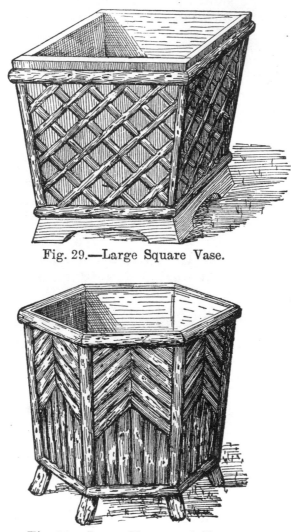

Fig. 29.—Large Square Vase.

Fig. 30.—Large Hexagonal Vase

structions. Split twigs are used for the fencing
around the shelves.

Fig. 29 shows a square vase constructed from
elm boards 1¼ in. thick. A fair size for the sides

will be 1 ft. 8 in. at the top and 1 ft. 5 in. at
the base by 2 ft. high, including the 2½-in. plinth.
The split twigs forming the decoration are 1½ in.
wide, and spaced about 2 in. apart edge to edge.
The vase shown by Fig. 30 is hexagonal in

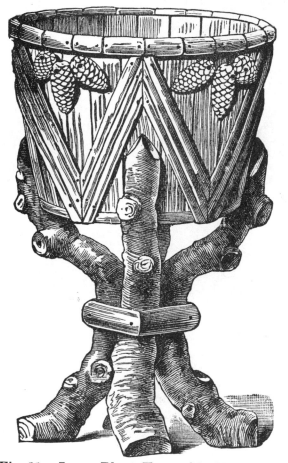

Fig. 31.—Large Plant Vase with Claw Foot.

shape, the sides being 1 ft. 8 in. high by 1 ft. 2 in.
wide at the top edge, and 1 ft. 0½ in. at the base.
The sides and bottom of both vases are connected
as in Figs. 21 and 22. Five 1-in. holes are bored
for drainage. The short feet having been secured

with screws driven from the inside, the split
rustic work is bradded on in the same order as
that described for Fig. 20.

The stands and vases should be given two
coats of oil varnish, allowing the first coat to
dry before applying the second.

A big plant vase made from half a paraffin
cask is illustrated by Fig. 31. An ordinary
40-gal. cask stands, roughly, some 3 ft. high, has
a diameter of some 2 ft., and is made of good
stout oak. Sawn through the middle, the paraf-

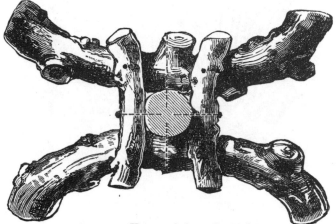

Fig. 32.—Foot of Rustic Table.

fin barrel makes two admirable tubs. One such
half is shown in Fig. 31. This it is proposed to
render suitable for some large bushy plant, so it
will have to be mounted on legs. The legs shown
are simply so many pieces cut from rough
branches. From a heap of stuff one can generally
choose pieces sufficiently adapted to the purpose,
though their exact contours will, of course, vary.
Oak branches, technically known as " bangles,"
from which the bark has been taken to make tan,
will do well; or if the bark is liked, apple-tree
or elm boughs will be suitable. That these sticks
should be rough and gnarled and knotted adds

to their effect. As the tub will be only partly covered with rustic mosaic work, it will be well before nailing anything upon it to paint it. A good dark brown or chocolate will go well with the natural bark. The rustic pieces will have to be cut through with the saw, the lengths being too great to be safely split with the hatchet—that is, with the exception of those round the lip, which are of thicker rod than the zig-zags; say, 1½ in. as compared with 1 in. In the zig-zags the light central strip is supposed to be of peeled

Fig. 33.—Garden Plant Tub.

withy, the darker ones on each side having the bark on, and being probably of hazel. Generally speaking, wrought brads are to be recommended for fixing rustic mosaic, but where, as in the present case, the strips have to be bent over a curved surface, small wire nails will be found more secure. Groups of fir cones, as shown, will prettily ornament the triangular spaces.

A style of foot suitable for a one-leg flower stand or table is illustrated in plan and part section by Fig. 32.

Fig. 33 shows the other half of the cask arranged for, say, a dwarf shrub, an orange-tree,

or the like.   In small town or suburban premises,
such tubs are specially useful where there is a
back court into which anything green cannot
otherwise be introduced.   In this, it will be seen
that by way of variety the tops of the staves
have been sawn to a zig-zag line, which is followed
a little below by a moulding of split rods.   Alternative styles of moulding are shown by Figs. 34
and 35.   Half-way between this and the bottom a
band of mosaic is arranged in light and dark
strips of withy and hazel.   The bits filling the

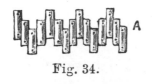 A

Fig. 34.

 B

Fig. 35.

Figs. 34 and 35.—Alterna-
tive Mouldings.   Fig. 36.—Ornamental Plant Vase.

diamond-shaped centres of this pattern are cut
from thicker stuff than the rest, so that they may
project as bosses beyond the general level.   Over
the unavoidable iron hoop at bottom, from which
place short strips would, if nailed, be often de-
tached, a rough "dry-cask" wooden hoop has
been fixed.   At the sides two pieces of rough
branch stuff have been placed to serve as handles,
and to resist strain these should be secured from
within by strong screws.

The vase shown by Fig. 36 is intended for a
somewhat low-growing flowering plant—say, a
large bushy geranium.   In its original character

it is an American lard pail. As in the last tub, the staves have been sawn to a more ornamental outline, and they have also been perforated. The ornamental strips of split rod have been arranged in straight vertical lines, to avoid the difficulty of bending and keeping them in place if bent round so small a vessel. The bottom of the pail is screwed down to an octagonal slab of wood, to the under side of which four short bits of rough bough are nailed as feet. As neither this

Fig. 37.—Rectangular Garden Plant Stand.

nor the last tub is wholly covered with mosaic, they should, of course, first be painted. The slab at bottom will look very well rough, as shown, but if painted it will be improved by strips of split rod nailed round its edges.

A garden plant stand, made from a soap box and mounted on legs is shown by Fig. 37. The easiest way to fix one of these legs on is to saw the piece of stuff in half to a distance from the top equal to the depth of the box, and then to cross-cut and remove one half. The corner of the box will be

brought to the middle of the cross-cut, and the leg
nailed on to the side of the box. The piece which
has been sawn off will then be cut through (quartered), and the proper quarter replaced and
nailed to the end of the box. Frets, such as those

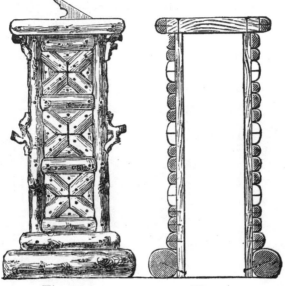

Fig. 38.   Fig. 39.

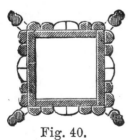

Figs. 38 to 40.—Elevation,
Section, and Horizontal
Section of Rustic Pedestal.

Fig. 40.

shown in these two examples, are patterns of a
kind well adapted to be worked out in rustic
mosaic.

A pedestal for a sundial or flower vase is
shown by Figs. 38 to 40. It is a box of 1-in.
elm boards, the top being a 2-in. thick slab.

Suitable dimensions are 3 ft. 6 in. high, and 1 ft. square, the top being 16 in. square.

A design for a rustic flower-pot stand in imitation of bamboo is represented by Fig. 41. The height should be about 2 ft. 6 in. to the top, and the length from 3 ft. to 3 ft. 6 in. The box at

Fig. 41.—Rustic Flower-pot Stand in Imitation of Bamboo.

the top may be about 9 in. wide and 8 in. deep. Care must be taken when putting the work together to get the frames true and square. Slovenliness in construction will completely spoil the appearance of the finished article. The box at the top is made to fit inside, and should be lined with a zinc tray. The outside may be covered with glue and brown sawdust.

CHAPTER III.

TABLES.

A SMALL rustic table which may, if desired, be used as a flower-pot stand, is illustrated by Fig. 42. The top may be made of $\frac{3}{4}$-in. stuff, and

Fig. 42.—Square Table.

should have two ledges nailed underneath to prevent twisting. The table may be 1 ft. 10 in. high, with the top 15 in. square, or, if a larger size is required, 2 ft. 1 in. high, with the top

18 in. square. The design is not suitable for tables of a larger size.

The legs may be secured to the top by boring holes in the ledges and driving them in. The cross bars must be firmly secured to the legs, and,

Fig. 43.—Hexagonal Table.

for the joints, the mortise and tenon shown at Fig. 6 (see p. 14) would be suitable. If the sticks used to form the legs are rather small, it will be better if the cross bars are kept a little higher on two of the sides, so that the mortises do not meet each other.

The top is covered with a Swiss overlay pattern, made of split sticks. The design may be set out by drawing lines from corner to corner on the top, and across the top in the centre of each side. A smaller square is then drawn in the centre of the top, with diagonals at right angles to the sides of the top. Lines drawn from the corners of the small square to the corners of the top will form a four-pointed star. The pattern should be clearly outlined with a pencil. In nailing on the sticks, those round the outer edge of the top should be put on first and mitred at the corners. Next the outside sticks of the small square should be nailed on, then the eight pieces

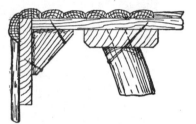

Fig. 44.—Part Vertical Section of Top of Hexagonal Table.

from the corners of the small square to the corners of the top.

In working up patterns of the above description, always nail on the sticks that follow the outline of the design first. The filling-in pieces may be put on afterwards. Variety may be given to the patterns by using sticks of different colours; for instance, the design may be outlined in hazel or blackthorn, and filled in with hawthorn or peeled willow. The edges of the table top are concealed by nailing on an edging of short sticks or cones.

Fig. 43 shows a small hexagon-top table for use in a summer-house or on the lawn. The following dimensions are suitable : Height 2 ft. 6 in., and diameter of circle for the hexagon top

2 ft. 9 in. The top is made from two or three $\frac{7}{8}$-in. boards cramped together to the required width and fixed underneath with two battens $3\frac{1}{2}$ in. wide by 1 in. thick. The four legs are dowelled and nailed to these battens and further stiffened by the rungs and the diagonal braces which are nailed to the legs. A corona is fixed

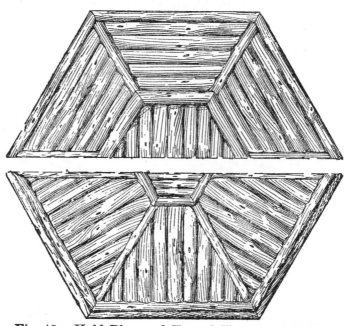

Fig. 45.—Half Plans of Top of Hexagonal Table.

around the edges of the table top, and the method of securing the board is shown in Fig. 44. In Fig. 45 the half plans show two ways of ornamenting the top. The twigs should be sawn so that in section they are less than a semicircle, and it will be an advantage to shoot their edges slightly, as then they will fit closer and cover the rough boards that form the table top.

CHAPTER IV.

CHAIRS AND SEATS.

For the armchair (Fig. 46) select four slightly curved legs about 3 in. in diameter; the front pair are 2 ft. high and the back pair are 2 ft. 9 in. high. The front seat rail is 1 ft. 2 in. long by

Fig 46.—Armchair

$2\frac{1}{2}$ in. in diameter, the back rail is 1 ft. long, and the side rails are 1 ft. 3 in. long, their ends being trimmed to fit the legs, and fixed with inserted ash or elm dowels $\frac{7}{8}$ in. in diameter; see Fig. 47. The height from the ground line to the seat top is 1 ft. 4½ in. The battens forming the seat rest on the side rails, and cleats are fixed to the inner sides of the four legs (see Fig. 48) to support the extreme back and front battens. The arms and back are made in three parts, the scarfed joints coming immediately over the back legs. The trellis work is then added, and finally the struts and dentils are fixed around the seat. The chair can be made from unbarked wood without any dressing, or the bark may be removed and

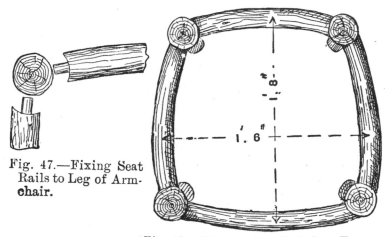

Fig. 47.—Fixing Seat Rails to Leg of Arm-chair.

Fig. 48.—Plan of Armchair Seat Frame.

the wood, when dry, can be finished in stain and outside varnish.

The garden-seats about to be described will look very effective if made of oak that has had the bark removed and the small twigs trimmed off clean; they should be finished in stain and varnish. In construction they are fairly simple.

For making the seat shown by Fig. 49, first select the three back posts, with their natural curves as much alike as possible. In diameter they should be from 2½ in. to 3 in. Select also two arm-posts and one centre leg for the front. Next cut two seat rails for the back and one rail for the front, 5 ft. or 6 ft. long as desired, and cut two side rails (see Fig. 50) and one centre rail, each 1 ft. 7 in. long. Work the ends of the rails to the shape of the posts as shown by Figs. 51 and 52, so that they make a fairly good joint, and bore the posts and rails with a $\frac{7}{8}$-in. bit $1\frac{1}{4}$ in. deep, to receive dowels made of ash or elm. These are preferable to tenons formed on the rails themselves. Now try the whole together tem-

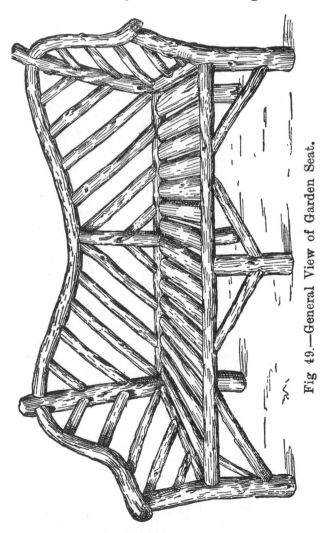

Fig 49.—General View of Garden Seat.

porarily, and make good any defects. Then take the pieces apart, and coat the joints with a thick priming consisting of two parts of white-lead (ground in oil) and one part of red-lead thinned with boiled linseed oil. Drive the joints home and fix them with nails or screws and wipe off

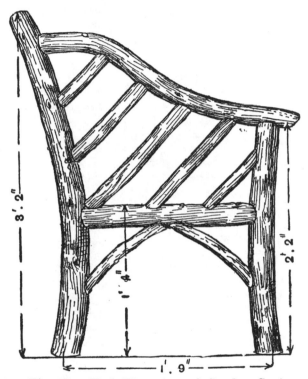

Fig. 50.—End Elevation of Garden Seat.

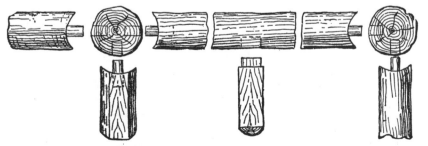

Fig. 51.—Joints of Rails and Posts for Garden Seat.

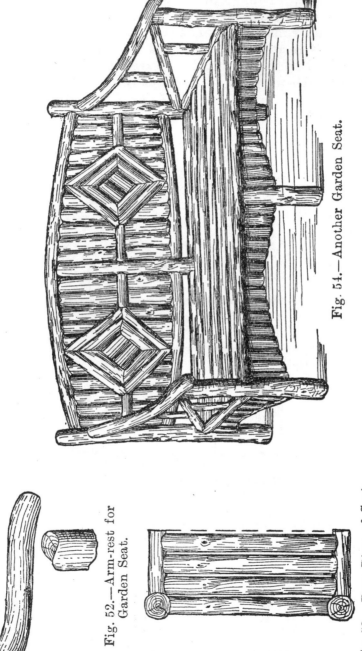

Fig. 54.—Another Garden Seat.

Fig. 52.—Arm-rest for
Garden Seat.

Fig. 53.—Part Plan of Seat.

the surplus paint. The top back rail and the arm-rest can next be fitted. The ends of the back rail are worked bird's mouth, to fit the posts. The arm-rests are treated in the same way at the back; they fit in vees cut in the front posts, and are fixed with nails.

Measure off and mark equal spaces for the

Fig. 56.—Vertical Section, showing Front Rail, Cross Rail, and Battens.

|← — — — 1. 9″ — — — →|

Fig. 55.—Cross Section of Garden Seat.

struts, the ends of which are trimmed to fit the rails and posts. Secure them with two nails at each end. The seat (Fig. 53) is made up of split saplings laid as shown, with the ends pared to fit the rails and bradded on. Finally, fit the struts between the seat rails and the lower part of the posts.

The framework for the chair shown by Figs.

54 and 55 is on the same principle as that already described.   The segmental battens forming the seat run longitudinally, and their ends are shaped to fit the outer rails.   The battens rest on a flat worked on the centre cross rail (see Figs. 55, 56, and 57).   Fig. 56 also gives a part cross section near the centre leg, and shows the front rail placed out of centre and the cross rail resting on the leg, to which it is firmly nailed.   When the seat is more than 5 ft. in length the battens require intermediate supports, which can be cut

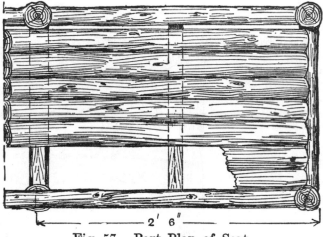

Fig. 57.—Part Plan of Seat.

from split saplings.   The panelling on the back is fixed to the top and bottom rails and supported in the centre by a wide longitudinal rail and two vertical rails at the mitres of the diamond centres.   These are fitted in and secured, and then the vertical split twigs are fixed partly on them and also on the rails.   Finally, struts are fixed to the seat rails and legs and covered with short twigs, with their lower ends running in a regular curve.

A rustic garden seat with canopy is illustrated by Fig. 58.   Where shade is required, the back and canopy offer facilities for securing it, as they can be covered with climbers. Fig. 58 is not drawn to scale, but the explanatory diagrams (Figs. 59 to 64) are ¾ in. to the foot.

The upright posts and all the more important pieces will best be formed of somewhat small larch stuff; the smaller straight sticks may be

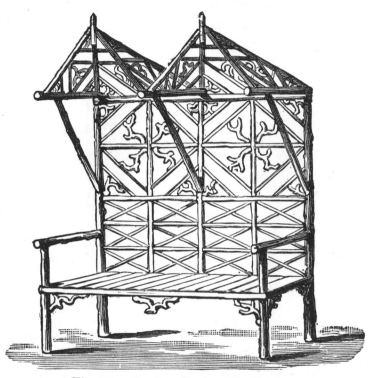

Fig. 58.—Garden Seat with Canopy.

hazel, birch, or withy. The last named, stripped of its bark, and used in some parts only, will form a pretty contrast with the darker rods. In filling spaces in back and canopy, a few pieces of crooked stuff are used; these will probably be of apple-tree.

The two posts A, on which almost the entire weight is sustained, should be let into the ground

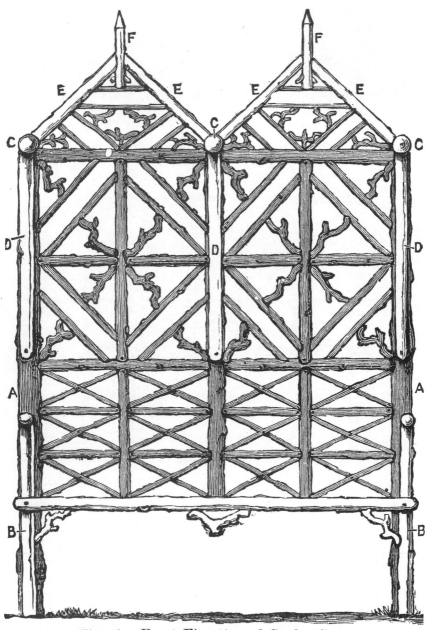

Fig. 59.—Front Elevation of Garden Seat.

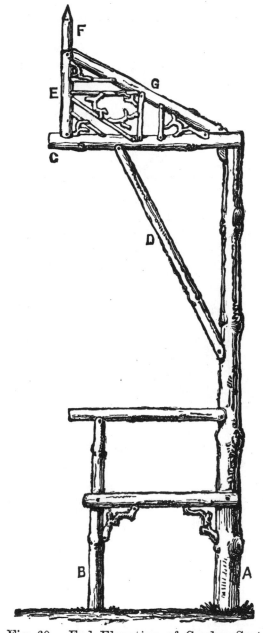

Fig. 60.—End Elevation of Garden Seat.

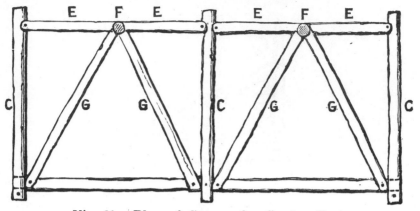

Fig. 61.—Plan of Canopy for Garden Seat.

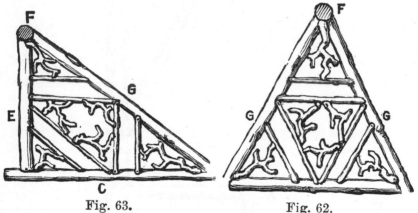

Fig. 63.   Fig. 62.

Figs. 62 and 63.—Back and Side Views of Canopy Panels.

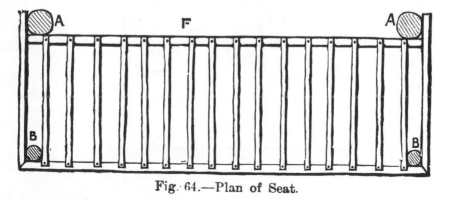

Fig. 64.—Plan of Seat.

not less than 2 ft. They rise 5 ft. above the
ground-line. They are set at a distance, measuring from centre to centre, of 4 ft. apart. The
smaller posts (marked B), which support the seat,
stand 17 in. in advance of those last named, and
should be let into the earth 1 ft. The broad seat
thus given is essential to comfort when the back
of the chair is upright, as it must be in this
instance.

Two principal **cross-pieces** are nailed against
the main posts. The lower one, of halved stuff,
is 15 in. from the ground, and carries the back
of the seat. The other is close to the top of the
posts, and carries the back of the canopy. The
canopy is chiefly supported on the three wall-
plates, C (Fig. 59), which rest at one end on the
heads of the posts, and towards the other on the
struts, D (Fig. 60). Fig. 61 shows in plan the arrangement of the principal pieces forming tne
canopy : E E are the rafters of the gables, the
lower ends of which rest on the wall-plates, and
the upper against the pinnacle, F (Fig. 61). The
back rafters are marked G G, and these rest their
lower ends on the cross-piece and their upper
against the pinnacle. Fig. 62 shows the filling-in
of the two back panels of canopy ; Fig. 63 that
of the four side panels.

The filling-in of the back of the seat is clearly
shown in Fig. 59.

In Fig. 64 the seat proper appears in plan.
Its front and ends are of halved stuff, nailed
to the posts. The spars forming the seat are
placed with spaces between them, that they may
not hold moisture ; for the same reason, it is
advised that they should be of peeled withy.

CHAPTER V.

GATES AND FENCES.

IN many gardens there is a space devoted to the tool-house, potting shed, refuse head, etc. Shrubberies of course hide the unsightly appearance

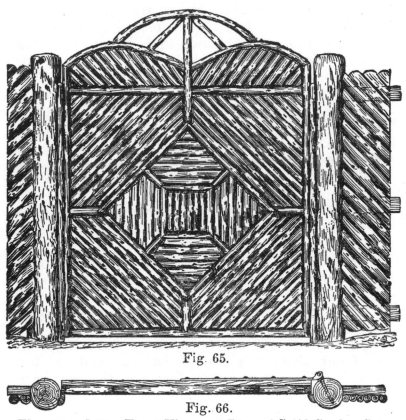

Fig. 65.

Fig. 66.

Figs. 65 and 66.—Front View and Plan of Solid Garden Gate.

of this particular spot to a certain extent, but it may be found desirable to close the entrance to this part of the garden from the remainder, and the gate illustrated in front elevation by Fig. 65

is, from its semi-rustic nature, particularly suitable. Fig. 66 shows a plan and Fig. 67 is a part
back view. The gate is quite simple in construc-

Fig. 67.—Part Back View of Frame for Solid Garden Gate.

tion, and should be of sufficient height to obstruct
the view from each side.

Local circumstances will of course determine
the width of the gate, but the one illustrated by

Fig. 65 is constructed on a framework 6 ft. square, the total height being 8 ft. The timber for the frame need not be planed.

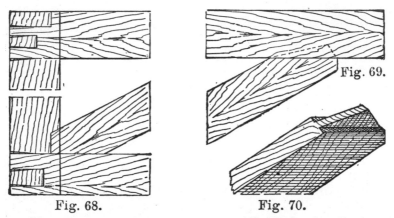

Fig. 69.

Fig. 68.   Fig. 70.

Figs. 68 to 70.—Joints in Frame of Solid Garden Gate.

Cut the closing and hingeing stiles 6 ft. long out of stuff 6 in. wide by $2\frac{1}{2}$ in. thick. The three rails are of the same dimensions, and can be halved and dovetailed to the stiles or, better, mortised, tenoned, and wedged and braced, as

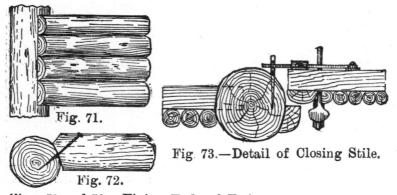

Fig. 71.

Fig. 73.—Detail of Closing Stile.

Fig. 72.

Figs. 71 and 72.—Fixing Ends of Twigs.

shown in Figs. 68, 69, and 70. Separate pieces of stuff are fixed up the centre to form a muntin for supporting the rustic work; the necessity is obvious from Fig. 66, where it will be noticed the twigs are outlined on the frame. Each twig has a bearing on the frame, and can thus be nailed individually.

Two stout gate hinges and hooks are required, and they can be bolted on with $\frac{7}{16}$-in. Whitworth bolts and nuts, or secured from the back with square-headed coach screws. Now commence fixing on the unbarked twigs; they should be as

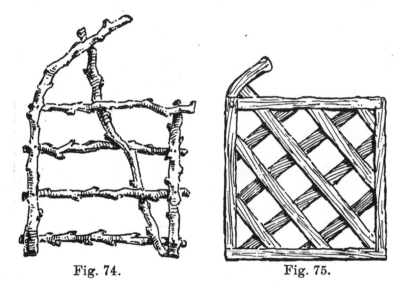

Fig. 74.   Fig. 75.

Figs. 74 and 75.—Designs for Rustic Gates.

straight as possible and used in their natural shape, without being split in halves.

The terminations of the joints for circular stuff are slightly different from the ends of the half-round stuff; see Figs. 71 and 72. Start by fixing the outside square, then the two inner squares, and finally the diagonal filling.

The posts are 9 in. or 10 in. in diameter by 9 ft. long, 3 ft. being underground. Cut three mortises in the posts to receive the rails for the side fencing. These rails are nailed flush to the secondary posts, nails also being driven through

each mortice in the gate posts. Next dig the
holes for the posts, these being kept at correct
distances apart by nailing battens to the top and
at the ground line while ramming in the posts.
Two parts of old brickwork and one part of
Portland cement will make a good concrete for
the posts.

A week or more should elapse before the gate
is hung to the posts. This may then be propped
up fair between the two posts, and the positions
should be marked for the staple of the latch,

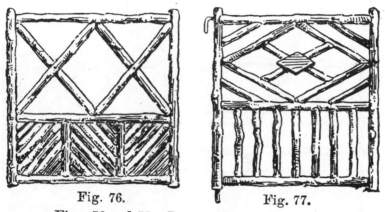

Fig. 76.   Fig. 77.

Figs. 76 and 77.—Designs for Rustic Gates.

and hooks for the hinges. A rebate is formed for
the gate on the posts by nailing on split sapling;
see Figs. 67 and 73. Finally, a short post can
be driven in the ground and fitted with a hook
for retaining the gate when open wide.

Suitable designs for small rustic gates are
given by Figs. 74 to 77. The wood for making
gates to the two designs (Figs. 76 and 77) should
have the bark removed. The chief rails and posts
are about 2 in. thick, filled in with 1½-in. or 1-in.
pieces, halved and nailed together where they
cross. The joints may be hidden by bosses of
planed wood (see Fig. 77). If the gate is to be
removable, fix a hook on the hanging stile to en-

gage with a staple in the joint, and a pin in the bottom to turn round in a socket. The gate is then easily taken out of its hangings. Varnish the wood on completion.

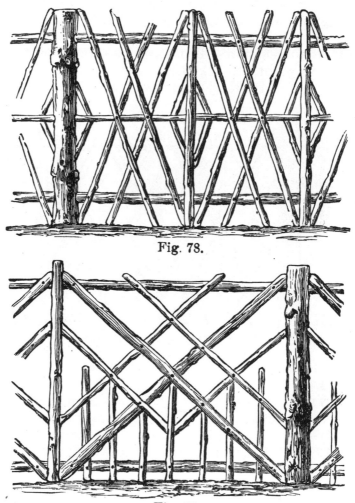

Fig. 78.

Fig. 79.

Figs. 78 and 79.—Designs for Fences.

Rustic fences can be constructed as shown in Figs. 78 to 80.

The garden trellis illustrated at Fig. 81 will

form an attractive addition to the grounds of a
suburban or country villa residence. In the case
of new houses, the existence of such a trellis,
with creepers ready planted, will often prove a
deciding factor in effecting a quick sale or letting.
The structure extends to a length of about 20 ft.,
but the dimensions may readily be altered to
suit requirements. The material may be fir or
other straight unbarked saplings and twigs. The
posts are 12 ft. long; the four for the arch being

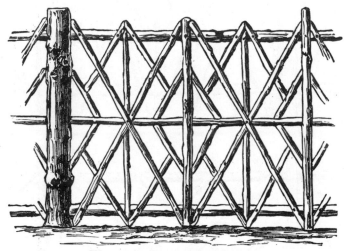

Fig. 80.—Design for Fence.

4 in. in diameter, and the others 3 in. or 3½ in.
The rails are 2½ in. in diameter, and the twigs for
the trellis, etc., 1¾ in. or 2 in. The bay seat with
canopy is 6 ft. long by 1 ft. 4 in. wide.

The position of the seats and posts and of the
shores A, B, and C is clearly shown in the plan (Fig.
82). The arrangement of the double posts adds
materially to the stiffness of the framework, making long shores unnecessary. The shores are
placed 3 ft. 6 in. above the ground line, and are
inclined at an angle of 50°. The posts are sunk
into the ground a distance of 3 ft., and well

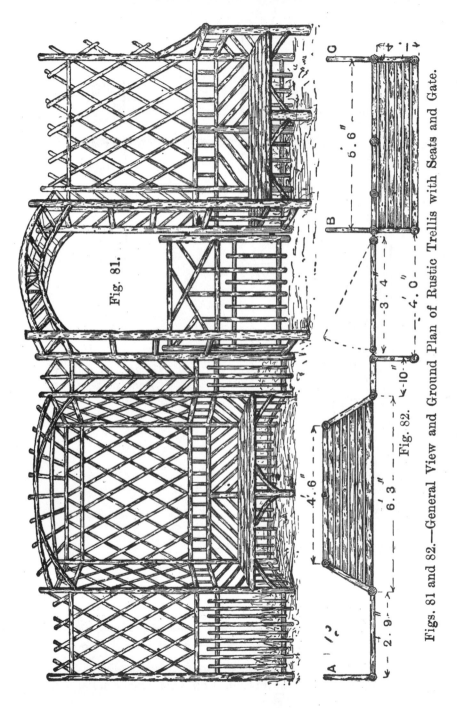

Fig. 81.

Fig. 82.

Figs. 81 and 82.—General View and Ground Plan of Rustic Trellis with Seats and Gate.

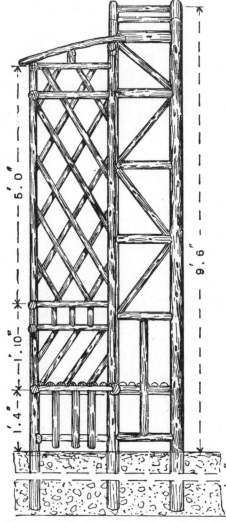

Fig. 85.—Detail of
Back of Seat for
Trellis.

Fig. 83.—Vertical Section of Trellis

Fig. 84.—Section through End Post and Trellis.

rammed in; rubble stones being mixed with the earth, as shown in the vertical section (Fig. 83).

The arch may with advantage be entirely fitted together before being put in position, as a better job can thus be made of the joints of the short rails and struts. The joints in the remainder of

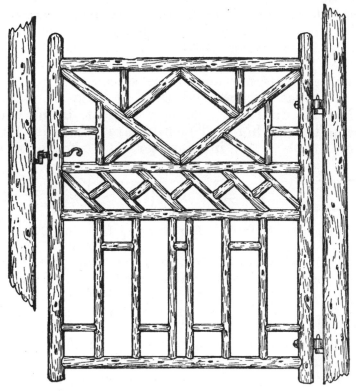

Fig. 86.—Alternative Design for Gate.

the work, with the exception of the gate, are of the simplest description. The rail ends are bevelled and notched to the posts, and secured with nails as shown in the sectional view of the trellis at Fig. 84.

Having erected the framework in position, next sink and well ram the shores deep into the ground, and splay and nail the top ends to the uprights. Also fix the shorter posts for the seats, letting them into the ground about 1 ft. 6 in. The end seat bearers are fixed to the end posts, and the centre bearers to the front and back central posts. The seat battens are saplings split in two, the flat portion being laid downwards and nailed to the bearers (see Fig. 83). Fig. 85 is an enlarged section through the seat back, showing the method of securing the smaller twigs to the rails. The fixing of the vertical pieces in the lower part, and the inclined lengths above, will complete this portion of the screen.

The gate, shown enlarged at Fig. 86, which gives an alternative design, is 3 ft. 9 in. wide by 4 ft. 6 in. high. The stiles are 4 ft. 9 in. long and about 2½ in. in diameter, and should be as

Fig. 87.—Method of Hanging and Latching Gate.

straight as possible, with the twigs neatly trimmed on; the rails should be at least 2¼ in. in diameter, trimmed to fit the stiles, and secured with inserted hardwood dowels 1 in. in diameter, as shown at Fig. 26, p. 27.

The diagonal struts in the top panel should be fitted and in place before the rails and stiles are finally secured; the vertical twigs in the lower panel should be similarly fitted and nailed before the rails are secured to the stiles. Ordinary forged hooks and eyes are used for hanging the gate; these are secured to the stile and post with nuts and washers, as shown in the enlarged horizontal section (Fig. 87).

A mortice is cut in the closing stile to receive the latch, the catch for the latter being a simple forging (see Fig. 88) with a pointed tang for driving into the post.

A rustic carriage entrance is shown by Fig. 89. The intention is, of course, that the rustic archway above the gates shall be more or less clothed with climbing plants. It is for roses that the structure will be best adapted, though clematis or honeysuckle will look well upon it. Ivy would look too heavy, and, if neglected, might even prove too heavy in other respects. Light as the arch may appear, the four posts grouped to form the turret on either side are so tied and braced together as to be, to all intents and purposes, a solid pillar, 30 in. square, and fully equal to resisting any outward thrust of the rafters. In the elevation (Fig. 89), to avoid confusion, no indication is given of the work forming the farther side of the arch, though something of it would

Fig. 88.—Catch for Gate.

necessarily be seen from the front; the two sides will be alike. Figs. 89 and 90 are drawn to a scale of ½ in. to the foot.

The posts, and at least all the more important straight pieces, should be of larch. The wood chosen for filling-in should have picturesque forks and contortions. Small oak bangles will, perhaps, be most appropriate.

In the ground plan of the left-hand turret (Fig. 90) it will be seen that the posts used—four at each end—are some 5 in. or 6 in. in diameter, and that the largest is selected as hanging-post for the gate. From centre to centre they are set 2 ft. 3 in. apart. They are 13 ft. long—that is, 10 ft. 4 in. above ground and 2 ft 8 in. below. The rafters of the arch spring from them 7 ft. from the ground, and at this point each post is surrounded by a cap, formed of four pieces of

quartered stuff nailed upon it. The rafters are
not mortised into the post, but if, instead of being
merely nailed, they are attached by a bolt and
nut, a stronger joint will be made.

The upper rafters, back and front, are con-

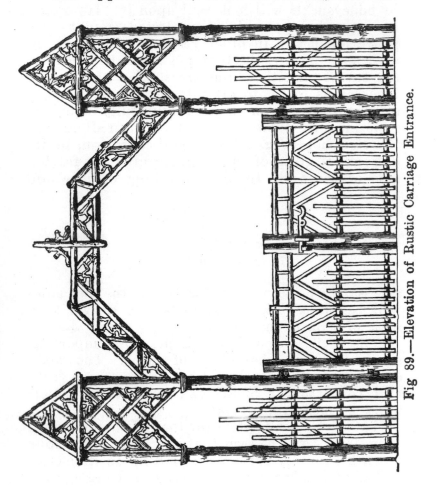

Fig 89.—Elevation of Rustic Carriage Entrance.

nected by five straight cross-pieces, whose ends
show in Fig. 89. The spaces between these are
filled up very much at random with crooked
stuff.

The four posts of each turret are bound together close beneath their tops by cross-pieces

nailed outside them, whilst from their tops, and nailed down to them, slant four short rafters, which meet pyramid-wise in the centre. The filling up of the upper parts of the turrets, as well as of the front and back of the arch, is with a mixture of straight and crooked stuff,

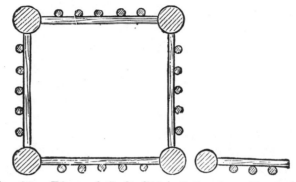

Fig. 90.—Plan of Left Side of Carriage Entrance.

the arrangement of which is clearly shown in the elevation (Fig. 89).

The lower parts of the turrets and the gates must be constructed in such a way as to exclude animals; the palings are so arranged as not to leave a space between them wider than 3 in. The rails of the gates should, of course, be mortised into the heads and hinge-trees.

CHAPTER VI.

ROSERY WALK.

THE rustic construction here illustrated is intended primarily as a trellis over which to train roses, and to form a shady and fragrant walk, and generally to contribute to the adornment of the flower garden. It can readily be adapted so as to form a roofed-in track from a door to the public roadway; and the means of so adapting it will be explained later.

The materials will be entirely rough wood in its natural bark. For the posts fir poles of some kind should be chosen, and larch is especially to be preferred both as regards durability and appearance. All the smaller pieces which show as straight stuff may well be of the same kind of wood as the posts, though hazel is best for the finer rods. It will be seen that in the mere filling-in much crooked stuff is used, and for this apple branches, or indeed almost anything that comes to hand, will answer

The rosery walk (Fig. 91) is 4 ft. wide, and the rustic erection is carried on two rows of pillars or collar-posts ranged at intervals of 3 ft. These posts should be let into the ground 2 ft., and well rammed in They should have an average diameter of 3 in. or $3\frac{1}{2}$ in., except in the case of each third one, as that which in Fig. 91 is seen standing in the middle of the portion with the lower roof; such pillars may be smaller as having little weight to bear, and will look better than they would do if equal in size to the others. Resting on the line of posts lies the wall-plate (A A, Fig. 92), the top of which is 5 ft. 6 in. from the ground line.

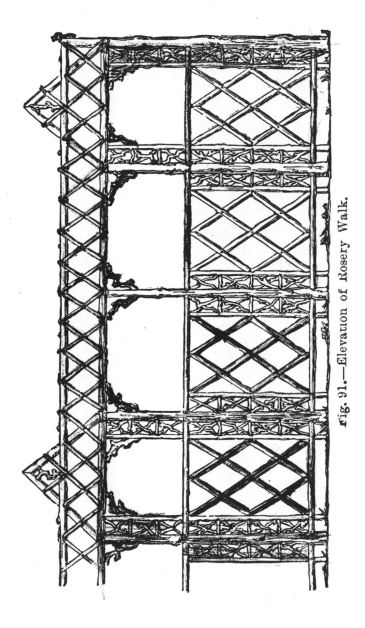

Fig. 91.—Elevation of Rosery Walk.

From each group of four large collar-posts rise four rafters (B, B, Fig. 92), meeting at top pyramid-wise. They rise to a height from the ground of 7 ft. 6 in., and have, therefore, to be 3 ft. 4 in. long. Half-way up them—that is, 6 ft. 6 in. from the ground line—the purlins (C, C, Fig. 92) are nailed upon them. Figs. 91

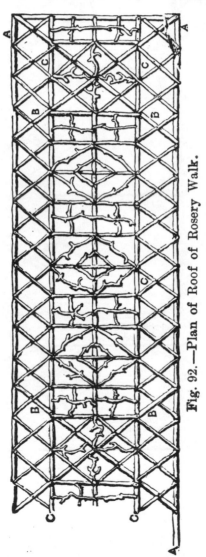

Fig. 92.—Plan of Roof of Rosery Walk.

and 92 alike show how the space between wall-plate and purlin is filled in, and Fig. 92 shows how the space, 7 ft. 3 in. long, stretching from one pyramidal portion to the next, is covered with a flat roof of open rustic work lying upon the purlins. This space, it will be observed, is chiefly filled in with crooked stuff.

Fig. 93 shows how the upper part of the rosery would appear at one of its ends, and explains how the roof would be in section—the shaded parts give the form of the roof in its lower portions; whilst if the cross-piece, D (which is on a level with the purlins), is supposed to be removed,

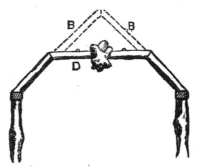

Fig. 93.—Entrance to Rosery Walk.

there is presented with the dotted lines, B, B, a section through the middle of one of the higher pyramidal portions.

Over the middle of the entrance is a rough knot or a piece of root.

The filling-in of the sides of the rosery is plainly shown in the elevation, Fig. 91. For its better preservation from damp, this work is kept 4 in. from the ground.

Supposing that, as was suggested above, the design is to be utilised for a dry path with a covering of metal or other light material, it will be well to keep the whole roof to the level of the pyramidal portions—a ridge-piece will have to be used—and the rafters, instead of following the present arrangement, will meet in pairs opposite to the pillars. Instead of round stuff, also, use halved stuff for the rafters and purlins, the sawn side being uppermost. The space between ridge-piece and purlin can then be filled in the same manner as that between purlin and wall-plate.

CHAPTER VII.

The rustic porch shown in front elevation by Fig. 94 and in vertical section by Fig. 95 is constructed from straight, well-seasoned saplings and twigs, from which, in each case, the bark has been removed. The design is eminently suitable for a farmhouse or a country cottage. The porch is of large dimensions, and is provided with seating accommodation on each side. The seats do not appear in the elevations, but one side is shown in the part plan (Fig. 96).

The seats are 1 ft. 6 in. high by 1 ft. 2 in. wide. The battens are $1\frac{3}{4}$ in. wide by $1\frac{1}{2}$ in. thick, and are supported on cross-pieces fixed to the front posts and wall; a centre batten being fixed to the centre panel, and supported by a diagonal bracket running from the front down to the sill-piece. The floor space is 7 ft. wide, and stands out 5 ft. from the walls.

The posts are 7 ft. 6 in. long by 4 in. in diameter. The front posts are preferably dropped over metal dowels leaded into the stone floor, at 1 ft. 2 in. centres, while the side posts are at $10\frac{1}{2}$ in. centres, and of smaller section—say about 3 in. in diameter. One post, 5 in. in diameter, sawn longitudinally through the centre, does duty for the two wall-posts, the flat portion being, of course, scribed to the wall, the latter having been previously plugged for the reception of the fixing nails.

The rails are tenoned to the posts, and $1\frac{1}{4}$-in. diameter holes are bored in the posts, and also in the ends of the rails, for the reception of the inserted tenons. The ends of the rails are also

hollowed to fit roughly the posts (see **Fig. 97**).
The lower rail is 10 in. up from the floor, while
the centre rail is 3 ft. 4 in. up.   The rail immediately below (Fig. 95) is 10 in. below the
centre rail.

The top ends of the front posts **are hollowed,**

Fig. 94.—Front Elevation of Cottage Porch.

and fitted with inserted dowels for the reception of the front rail. The six side-posts are finished off square, and have tenons which fit into the plates. The front ends of the plates are notched to the front top rail. The rafters are 5 ft. 7 in. long by 3 in. deep and 2 in. wide, wrought and

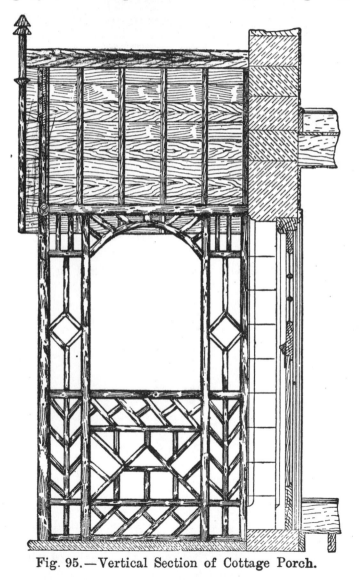

Fig. 95.—Vertical Section of Cottage Porch.

chamfered and birdsmouthed to the plates as
shown at Fig. 98. The ridge piece, 4 in. deep
by 1½ in. thick, projects 5 ft. 2 in. from the wall.
On the front end of the ridge is fixed the finial,

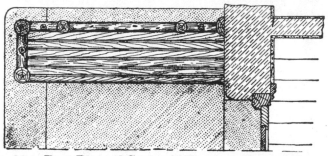

Fig. 96.—Part Plan of Seat and Floor of Cottage Porch.

which is 2 in. square. The rafters are covered
with 1-in. V-jointed, wrought, grooved and tongued boarding, cut in 5-ft. 4-in. lengths, and laid
horizontally or at right angles to the rafters.

The roof may be covered with slates, with
Broseley tiles, with wood shingles, or with thatch.
A part plan of the roof is shown in Fig. 99. An

Fig. 97.—Section of Cottage Porch at Gable.

enlarged section of the front angle of the gable
is given in Fig. 100. Two boards, each 1 ft. 1 in.
wide by 1¼ in. thick, are fixed to the outer rafters
and run parallel with them; the heels of the two

boards abutting on the front top rail, to which they are nailed The split-twig herringbone ornament is also nailed to these boards. On the inner edges of the boards are secured twigs of about

Fig. 98.—Enlarged Detail of Cottage Porch at Eaves.

1¾-in. in diameter, which are rebated to fit to the edges as shown in Fig. 100. The front projecting ends of the roofing boards are concealed by split twigs of about 2½-in. or 3-in. diameter, which do

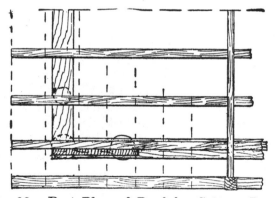

Fig. 99.—Part Plan of Roof for Cottage Porch.

duty as bargeboards. The method is shown at A (Fig. 100).

The panels have now to be filled with stuff ranging from 1½ in. to 2¼ in. in diameter. The

vertically placed twigs between the posts and rails
should be fitted in place before the rails are finally jointed up to the posts. The ends are roughly
hollowed, and are secured with cut nails. Alter-
natively, the vertical members could be fitted so
that their inner edges coincided with the centre
of the rails. The major portion of the twigs
being on the outer side, the smaller diameter of
the twigs will thus bring their front edges flush
with the larger diameter edges of the rails. The

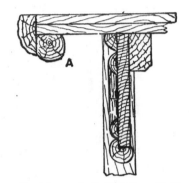

Fig. 100.—Section of Gable for Cottage Porch.

herringbone and the diagonally placed twigs are
quite easy to fit, the ends being simply pared off
till they are sufficiently shortened to assume their
correct position in the panels.

The decorative effect of the porch will be
greatly improved by the addition of a suitable
door, as shown in the front elevation (Fig. 94).
The cost of manufacture of such a door is but
slightly more than that of an ordinary six-panel
door. The bottle ends in the top glazed panel
form a quaint and pleasing feature of the general
scheme.

CHAPTER VIII.

CANOPY FOR A SWING.

FIG. 101 is a general view of the canopy and swing, and Fig. 102 a side elevation slightly more elaborate in design than Fig. 101, the chief members, however, being exactly the same. The

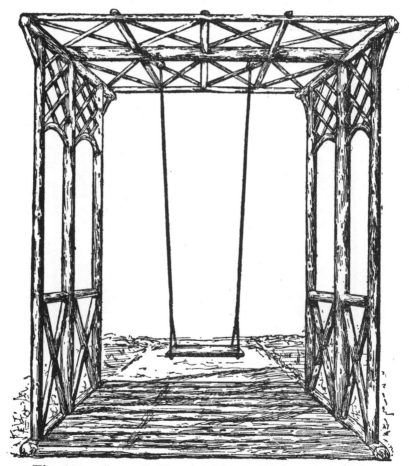

Fig. 101.—General View of Rustic Canopy for Swing.

material used is stripped fir saplings. Six **of** these are required for the uprights.

The middle posts are slightly larger in section, as they have to carry the cross rail supporting the swing; a good size for these is 6-in. diameter

Fig. 102.—Side Elevation of Canopy for Swing (Alternative Design).

at the base by 10 ft. or 12 ft. high. The out**er** posts may be $4\frac{3}{4}$-in. to 5-in. diameter at the base. The posts are sub-tenoned (see Fig. 103) to elm sills 10 ft. 6 in. long by 8 in. diameter. Tenons **are** formed on both ends of the posts, and **seatings**

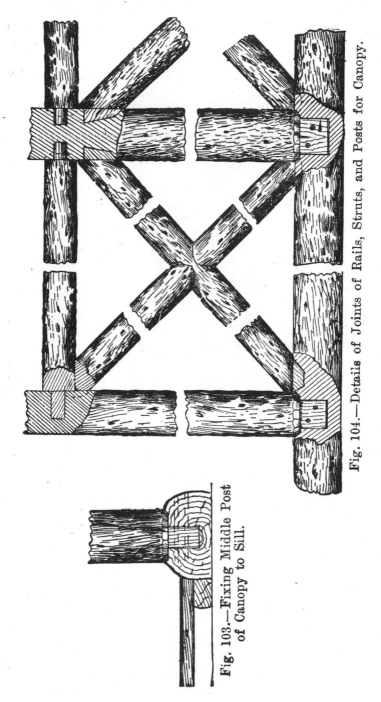

Fig. 104.—Details of Joints of Rails, Struts, and Posts for Canopy.

Fig. 103.—Fixing Middle Post of Canopy to Sill.

and mortices at 4-ft. centres are made in both the
sills (bottom rails) and plates (top rails) to receive them.

The short rails are 4 in. in diameter by

Fig. 105.—Securing Cross Rails to Plates and Posts of
Canopy.

3 ft. 6 in. long, and are stub-tenoned and pinned
to the posts at a height of 3 ft. 9 in. from the
ground line. The struts also are tenoned and
pinned to the middle posts and sills, as shown
in Fig. 104, where, it will be noticed, the struts

Fig. 106.   Fig. 107.

Figs. 106 and 107.—Hook and Thimble for Canopy.

are in one piece and the braces in two, the latter
being hollowed to fit in the angles and over the
struts.

When all the members are ready for the final

drive home, the tenons of the rails should be just
entered to the posts; the struts and braces are
next placed in position and driven up, then the
sill and plate are entered and driven home, and

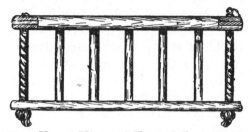

Fig. 108.—Front View of Fenced Seat for Canopy.

finally the several joints are secured with oak
pins. This operation will be carried out better
with the work in a horizontal position. When the
two sides are so far completed, they may be
erected in position and fixed with temporary battens, at a distance apart of 7 ft. 9 in. centres,
while the top cross rails are being fitted.

Fig. 110.—Fixing Rope
to Eyelet.

Fig. 109.—End View of
Fenced Seat for Canopy.

The middle cross rail which carries the swing
is 6 in in diameter and 8 ft. 6 in. long. A seating is formed on the plates, and a shallow one
upon the rails, which are secured with long ¾-in.

diameter bolts and nuts; the latter are let into
the posts at a distance of 8 in. from the top, as
shown in Fig. 105, which is a cross section through
the plate near the middle rail. Short struts may
also be fixed between the posts and cross rail, as
in Fig. 105; they are not shown in Fig. 101. A
floor is formed of saplings, connected to the sills,
thus preventing them from spreading. The trel-
lis-work, both on the roof and sides, is now fixed.
This is composed of $1\frac{3}{4}$-in. and 2-in. twigs.

The swing hooks (Fig. 106) pass right through
the rails, and are secured with nuts and washers.
Collars should be forged on the shanks to prevent
the hooks being drawn too far into the wood
when screwing up the nuts. The shank is screwed
$\frac{3}{4}$-in. Whitworth pitch thread, and the hook is
$1\frac{1}{4}$ in. in diameter at the thickest part. The hemp
rope is spliced around galvanised iron thimbles
(see Fig. 107), which take the wear on the hooks.
The rope is usually secured to the seat by simply
knotting the ends.

Should the swing be used for very young
children, a seat provided with a fence will be
necessary, as shown at Figs. 108 and 109, which
are front and end views respectively. The back
rail and the two side rails are fixed to the seat
with the balusters; but the front rail is tenoned
to open-ended mortices in the side rails, and thus
made to hinge, to facilitate the lifting of the
children on and off the seat, the rail being secured
in its closed position with a brass pin and retaining chain. The suspending rope in this case is
passed through the end rails and knotted to the
seat. Fig. 110 shows the rope passed around and
whipped to an eyelet.

CHAPTER IX.

AVIARY.

THE outside dimensions of the rustic aviary shown by Figs. 111 and 112 are—length, 3 ft. 2 in.; width, 1 ft. 6 in.; height, 1 ft. 10 in.

Hazel sticks, with the bark on, should be used, the straightest obtainable being best for the frame; if at all crooked or bent, the sticks can be straightened by steaming, or, if not too dry, by the heat of a spirit lamp.

Four uprights, 1 ft. $5\frac{1}{2}$ in. by $\frac{5}{8}$ in., are first cut; then six rails, $\frac{1}{2}$ in. thick, are made, with the ends shaped as shown in Fig. 113, to fit the uprights, measuring 2 ft. 10 in. inside the hollow ends when finished. Four of these should be laid on the bench side by side, and marked with a pair of compasses for the wires, which are $\frac{5}{8}$ in. apart. They are then drilled, the holes being bored right through the two sticks for the top rails, but only half through the bottom rails. If the stuff is not too hard, the holes may be pierced with a well-sharpened bradawl.

The uprights are now secured to the rails with 2-in. wire nails, driven so as to avoid the holes (see Fig. 114), and glue is applied at the joints. The bottom rail is flush with the lower ends, the next one being placed $1\frac{1}{2}$ in. above it; the third is $\frac{1}{4}$ in. from the top ends. These form the front and back frames, and should be quite square and out of winding. The rails for the ends, also six in number, measure 1 ft. 3 in., and are bored and fixed to the uprights to correspond with the others in exactly the same way.

The two rails supporting the tree perches are placed about 7 in. from the ends. Before they

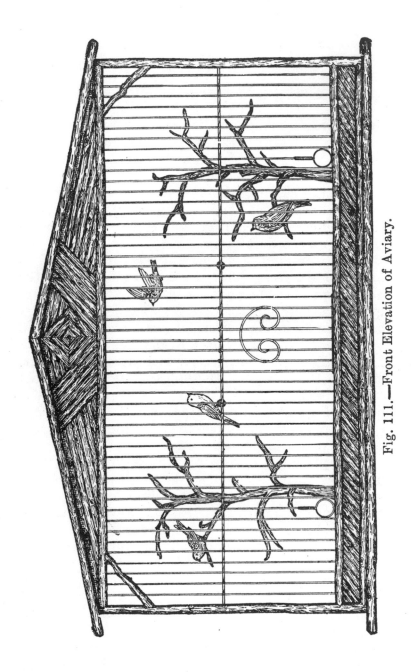

Fig. 111.—Front Elevation of Aviary.

are fixed, however, the tree perches must be arranged. These should be cut from the limb of a leafless tree, in winter, in order to retain the bark

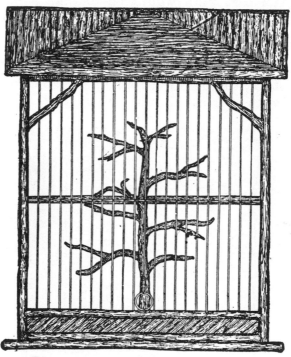

Fig. 112.—End Elevation of Aviary.

Suitable pieces may be prepared by cutting off badly placed twigs and fixing them where required. They are then put on the perch rails,

Fig. 113.   Fig. 114.

Figs. 113 and 114.—Details of Joint of Rails and Uprights for Aviary.

employing the same joint as the rails and upright, but securing with a strong screw.

When all is ready, the perches are fixed in the framework (see Figs. 115 and 116), and narrow strips of ¼-in. board are fitted between the lower rails of the back and ends, to be faced with split stuff, put on diagonally as shown in Figs. 111 and 112. The best plan would be to take a sufficient quantity of material to the nearest sawmill to be divided by a circular or band saw; the material must be free from grit, or objections will be raised against cutting it.

A stain, made by thinning down brunswick black with turps, should be at hand to stain

Fig. 115.—Part Sectional Plan of Aviary.

the wood before fixing on the split stuff, which is secured with fine panel pins.

The wood bottom is 3 ft. 1½ in. by 1 ft. 5½ in. by ⅜ in.; it is planed both sides, and secured in place with screws. The top side is treated round the margin, as shown in Fig. 115, and the under side as shown in Fig. 117. The centre of the design of the under side, covering a space of 2 ft. 3 in. by 8 in., is worked first; it is worked from the centre outwards, each strip being mitred as shown. The marginal strips are pieces of split cut slanting at the ends where they fit other pieces, and flush with the edge of the wood bottom, which is surrounded with the same stuff.

The wiring is all straightforward work. The wires are passed through the top rails to those below and clipped off level at the top. Six feeding-holes are required, one in the centre at each

Fig. 116.—Cross Section of Aviary.

end, and two at the back and front close to the perches. The top ends of these wires are pushed up through the rails; the circular ends are slightly sunk and fixed with small staples. Six wires are omitted from the middle of the front to allow for the door. The cross-wires, which should be of a stronger gauge, are then put in. In the back and ends it is immaterial whether

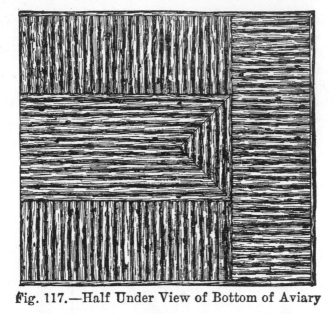

Fig. 117.—Half Under View of Bottom of Aviary

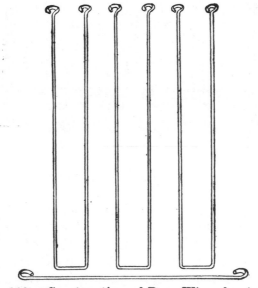

Fig. 118.—Construction of Door Wires for Aviary.

they are put inside or out, but at the front they must be inside. The six wires above the door are inserted in twos, being returned in the same manner as the lower ends of the door wires (see Fig. 118), and soldered to the cross-wire, which is afterwards bound to the others with thin pliable coil wire. In making the sliding door, the returned ends of the wires are soldered to the base

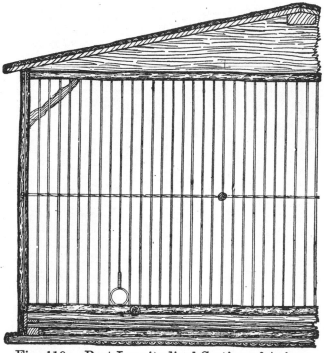

Fig. 119.—Part Longitudinal Section of Aviary.

wire inside, so that the ends may fit round the wires of the doorway; the top ends fit round those above the cross-wire, and when the door is in place a scroll-piece is soldered on outside (see Fig. 111).

Eight corner-pieces of the split stuff are put on close against the wires, being secured to the uprights and rails with pins. Two pieces of ¼-in

board are next got out for the top, measuring
2 ft. 10 in. long, 4 in. across the centre, and
slanting at the upper edge to ¼ in. at the ends.
The design is worked on these in split, the boards
being kept in place with pins driven through the
top rails, and the back and front connected at the
top point by a length of wood of 2-in. by 1-in.
section (see Fig. 119). The roof-pieces, 1 ft. 5½ in.

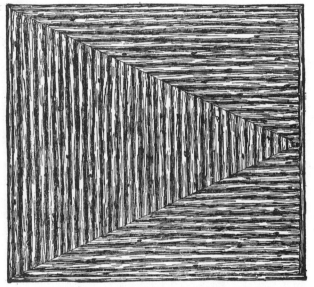

Fig. 120.—Half Plan of Aviary Roof.

by 1 ft. 7¼ in. by ¼ in., are nailed on and covered
with split stuff, as shown by Fig. 120.

A sliding bottom or tray is required for clean-
ing purposes; this is of ¼-in. board, and is nailed
to the strip that fits between the rails in front;
other strips about 1 in. wide are nailed on the
upper side at the extreme ends and back edge
to form a tray for the sand, runners being put in
against the lower end rails. The front strip is
treated with the split, and to draw out the tray,
the door may be slightly raised to admit the fin-
gers to push it forward from the inside. Two

additional perches put across from the wires, and fixed with staples, give strength to the front and back.

The aviary is now gone over with fine glass-paper, all white places being touched up with the stain and nicely varnished, with the exception of the perches. The aviary will stand on a table, but may be hung from the ceiling if desired. For hanging purposes, four screw-eyes are put in the top, two on the ridge, about 3 in. from the front and back, and one towards each end, placed midway to catch the rails. The four ceiling hooks should screw into the joists, the aviary being suspended with chains.

CHAPTER X.

FOOT-BRIDGES.

VERY pleasing effects may be produced in public or private recreation grounds by the constructional use of rustic work of good design.

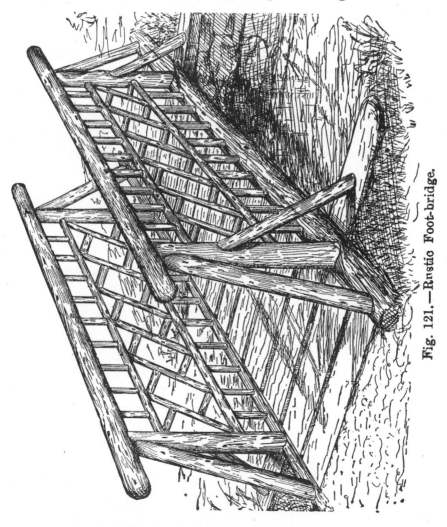

Fig. 121.—Rustic Foot-bridge.

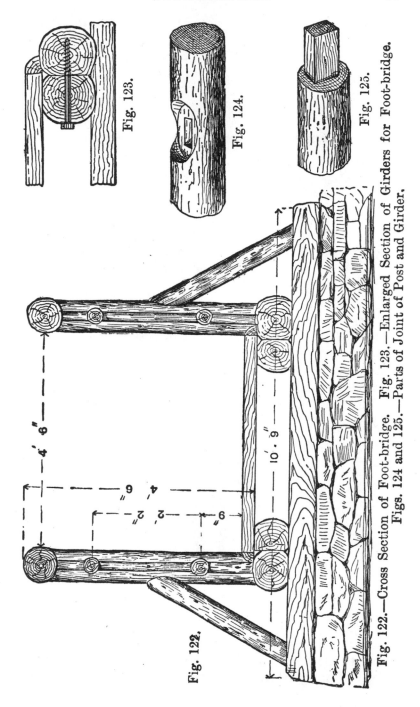

Fig. 123.

Fig. 124.

Fig. 125.

Fig. 122.

Fig. 122.—Cross Section of Foot-bridge. Fig. 123.—Enlarged Section of Girders for Foot-bridge.
Figs. 124 and 125.—Parts of Joint of Post and Girder.

Fig. 121 is a perspective view of a rustic foot-bridge suitable for a span of 8 ft. or 12 ft. The banks of the stream to be bridged are excavated to allow of the building of a low rubble wall, on

Fig. 126.

Fig. 128.

Fig. 127.

Fig. 126.—Detail of Middle Rail and Post of Foot-bridge.
Figs. 127 and 128.—Joint of Strut to Post of Foot-bridge.

which the sleepers rest, as shown in Fig. 122. The girders are formed of spruce or larch spars. In the present instance, four are used; and they may be 8 in. or 10 in. in diameter, according to

Fig. 129.—Twig Hollowed to fit Rail of Foot-bridge.

the length of the span. They are roughly adzed down to sit on the sleepers, and each girder is also worked down tolerably flat on the inner sides. The girders are then bolted together in pairs with six $\frac{3}{4}$-in. diameter coach bolts, as shown by Fig. 123. The posts are tenoned and wedged to fit mortices in the girders. Figs. 124 and 125 show the mortice and tenon joint.

The posts and top rails are $4\frac{1}{2}$ in. or $5\frac{1}{2}$ in. in

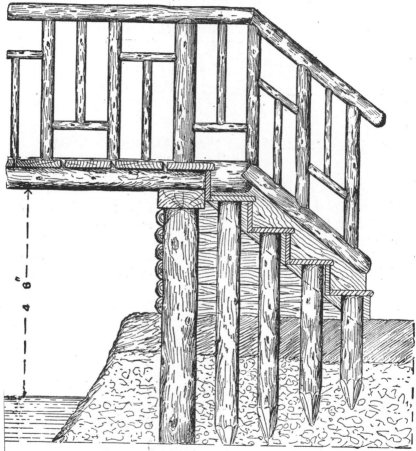

Fig. 130.—Elevated Foot-bridge.

diameter, and the intermediate rails 3 in. in diameter. Fig. 126 indicates the method of jointing the rails to the posts. The girder spars, with posts and rails fitted, having been placed in position on the sleepers, and plumbed up and stayed, the floor battens, 11 in. by $2\frac{1}{2}$ in.,

are fixed and the struts are fitted and pinned **or**
spiked to the posts and sleepers. The joint **for**
the struts is shown by Figs. 127 and 128.

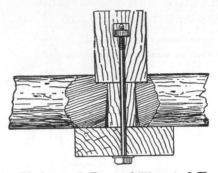

Fig. 131.—Girder and Post of Elevated Foot-bridge
Bolted to Sleeper.

If the bridge happens to be in a locality that
is subject to periodical flooding, it should be
anchored to prevent its being unseated by flood
water. The anchoring can be best effected by
driving four short piles into the soil on the inside
of both girders and near their ends.   The girders

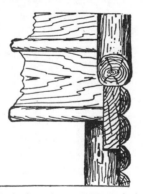

Fig. 132.—Cross Section of Elevated Foot-bridge
at Lower Step (Fig. 130).

can be fastened to the piles with coach bolts.
The tops of the piles will be concealed by the end
floor battens.   The smaller twigs forming the

ornamentation are now fixed, and Fig. 129 shows the vertical piece hollowed to fit the rails.

Fig. 130 gives a part view, in longitudinal section, of an elevated bridge, suitable for a span of 12 ft. to 18 ft., and raised on piles to enable small boats and canoes to pass under. Elm logs are suitable for the pile foundation. An iron ring must be fitted over the tops of the logs while they are being driven, and it will be necessary to use a pile-driver. The logs, having been sufficiently driven, are cut off to the required height from the ground line. Three piles on each side are required to carry the sleepers. The bridge is 5 ft. 6 in. wide, and the spars for girders are 12 in. in diameter. The sleepers are bolted to the piles, and the girders are also bolted to the sleepers as shown by Fig. 131. A row of smaller piles is now driven, and a plank, 11 in. by 3 in., is housed to the top ends of these piles, and also connected to the projecting ends of the girders. The treads of the steps rest upon the tops of the smaller piles, and the outer side of the piles and planks is covered with split saplings (see Fig. 130, and the cross-section, Fig. 132). The handrails and balustrades are fixed in similar manner to those in Fig. 121.

CHAPTER XI.

VERANDAHS.

THE front elevation of a rustic verandah is presented by Fig. 133, which shows a part only, which may be extended to any required length at either end. As to the width, that indicated is 3½ ft. from the wall to the middle of the collarposts, the eaves having a further projection of 6 in. For a cottage verandah the width given is a satisfactory one. It gives sufficient room for seats on a hot day, or for a promenade on a wet one. The width, as also the height, can easily be increased to suit a larger house. The verandah is supposed to be built on a raised platform of brick or stone.

All parts of the actual framework are of straight natural wood, preferably larch; whilst the mere filling-in of rustic open-work is of small crooked stuff—probably oak or apple tree. The roof, as illustrated, is of tiles.

It will be seen that the posts which support the verandah are arranged in pairs, so that 3 in. or 3½ in. poles will suffice for them. Their bases are supposed to be dowelled to the masonry of the platform on which they stand; they are 6 ft. 6 in. high. Except at the entrances, a sill of half-stuff runs from post to post on the platform. At a height of 3 ft. 3 in. they are connected by a round bar of smaller material, and, again, by a second cross-bar of similar size to the last, at 6 in. from their upper ends. On the tops of the posts rests a lintel of half-stuff of larger diameter—say 5 in. The upper and lower cross-bars come opposite to the middles of the posts, but need not be mortised into them, for if their ends are cut V-shaped, so as to clip the posts, they can be nailed quite firmly. The lower cross-rail is placed at a convenient height for

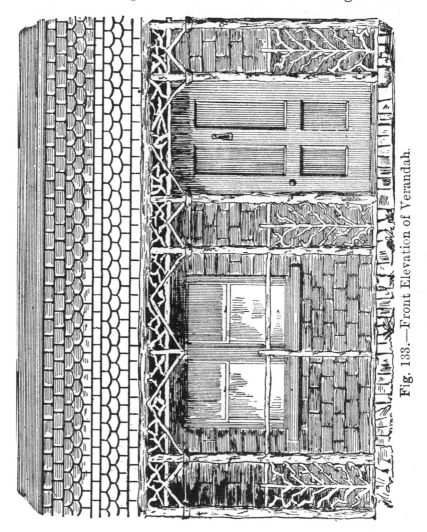

Fig. 133.—Front Elevation of Verandah.

leaning upon. At a height of 5 ft. 6 in. caps are formed by simply nailing four pieces of quartered stuff round each post. The diagonal braces which start from above the capitals pass in front of the upper cross-bars, to which and to the

lintel they are nailed. Fig. 133 sufficiently
shows how the panels between the pairs of posts
and the frieze between the upper cross-bar and
lintel are filled with open-work of small crooked
branches, which contrasts in a pleasing manner
with the straight pieces of the framework. This
open-work may be made available for, and will
be found useful as, a support for climbing plants.

In so narrow a structure the rafters alone will
suffice to keep all in place, without anything of
the nature of a tie-beam being called for. These
rafters will be of half-stuff, and for the given
width a length of 5 ft. will be enough; this will
allow of such a projection beyond the lintel as
will give the eaves a width of 6 in.; the pitch will
be rather less than a true pitch, but amply steep
for the purpose. A piece of half-stuff nailed to
the wall will support the upper ends of the
rafters.

In forming the roof it is proposed to board
over the whole space upon the rafters, and to
nail the tiles or other covering upon the boards.
The inside may be lined beneath the boarding with
rush matting. This is an inexpensive material;
its brownish-green hue is pleasing to the eye, and
it is so inartificial in appearance as to harmonise
well with the natural wood. After fixing the
rafters, the matting is to be stretched tightly
across them before the boards are nailed down. It
is probable that the rafters will be arranged with
intervals of about a foot between them, and to
hold the matting more closely to the boards a
strip of split rod may be nailed up the middle
of each space, or strips may be nailed so as to
form a simple ornamental pattern; an intricate
one will not be desirable, as fixing it will be over-
head work.

A neat, but less characteristic, ceiling may be
formed by painting the boards a suitable colour
and slightly ornamenting them with split strips

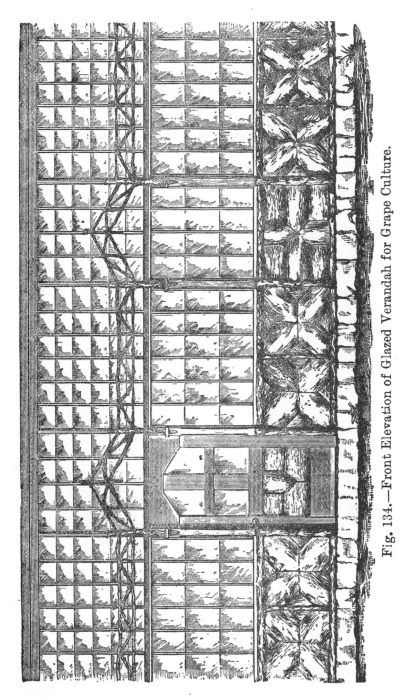

Fig. 134.—Front Elevation of Glazed Verandah for Grape Culture.

of rod. In this case the boards should be planed.
None will be better for this purpose than ¾-in.
flooring boards, and these are commonly sold
planed on one side. Other ways of lining the
roofs of rustic buildings are discussed in Chapter
XIII. For summer-houses thatch makes a good-
looking roof, but a thatched verandah would
scarcely be desirable unless attached to a
thatched cottage. Practically the choice lies between shingles, metal, and tile or slate. A metal
roof is, undoubtedly, that most easily fixed by the
beginner; black sheet iron looks better than galvanised, and must be kept painted. As a matter
of taste, metal looks thin and poor, but it be-
comes less objectionable when painted; a deep,
dull red would be the colour to be preferred.
Perhaps, of all available coverings, nothing will
look better than tiles, as drawn. Red or buff
tiles will in themselves look best, but the choice
must, to an extent, be influenced by the general
covering of the house. It may be, if that is of
slate, that small slates will come in most appro-
priately; but whichever of these coverings is used,
the best finish against the wall will be with a
" flashing " of metal, as shown.

It has been asserted by some who consider
themselves authorities in matters of taste that
nothing of the nature of a greenhouse ever har-
monises with natural surroundings, or is otherwise than an eyesore in a garden in other respects beautiful. The hard, straight lines of wood
or metal, and wide surfaces of shining glass, are
not pleasing, and are too suggestive of the shop
and factory to accord well with natural objects.
It has been suggested that the difficulty might be
overcome by combining rustic work with glass.
This, at the first glance, looks fairly easy; but, on
consideration, it will be seen to be otherwise. Rustic carpentry is in its nature irregular, and cannot be brought to those level planes and straight

lines essential to glass-work; whilst for interiors, and especially those of houses intended for vines, rough bark-coloured surfaces afford too much shelter to insect pests—so that, in reality, rustic-work can only be made applicable to a very

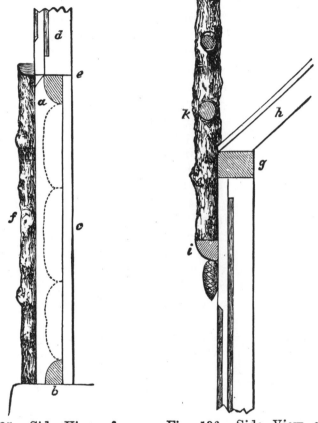

Fig. 135.—Side View of Bottom of Post for Glazed Verandah.

Fig. 136.—Side View of Top of Post for Glazed Verandah.

limited extent. In the grape-growing verandah shown by Fig. 134, therefore, only a limited amount of rustic-work has been introduced, and that on the outside.

Such of the materials as are of a rustic kind

are, for the parapet and uprights, some rather small larch poles or other tolerably straight, round stuff, and for the panels, some of those " slabs," or rough outside planks. As to the posts, and such parts as are not rustic, they are supposed to be of good deal. The sash-bars, which carry the glass both in roof and walls, are to be bought struck by steam at a lower price than they can be worked by hand, or sashes may be bought ready glazed. For glazing work of this kind, 16-oz., or sometimes 20-oz., glass is used.

As in the design for an open rustic verandah (see Fig. 133) it is intended that the collar-posts should be set upon and dowelled into a raised platform of masonry. The present structure is, of course, intended for the warmer sides of a house, south or west. The width, to meet particular cases, can be varied, but is, according to the drawings, $4\frac{1}{2}$ ft. The posts are 6 ft. high and $3\frac{1}{2}$ in. square. They are set with spaces between them alternately of 3 ft. and $4\frac{1}{2}$ ft. On their tops rests a wall-plate of the same width as themselves, and $2\frac{1}{2}$ in. deep. The rafters, which are sash-bars rebated to carry the glass, rest on this wall-plate, and against a second vertical one fixed to the house wall.

Fig. 134 is a front elevation of a portion of the verandah, whilst Fig. 135 gives a side view of the lower half of one of the collar-posts. At a, in Fig. 135, is seen the section of the upper cross-rail, which has its top $2\frac{1}{2}$ ft. from the ground; at b is the lower cross-rail, or sill. Both are of quartered rough stuff, and are mortised to the post $\frac{3}{4}$ in. from its inner edge, so that when the $\frac{3}{4}$-in. boarding, c, is nailed against them, it will come flush with the inner side of the post. At d is indicated the sash-frame, with its rebate for glass, which occupies the upper part of the opening; and at e is a metal flashing between rail and sash to throw off rain. It is proposed that the sashes in the narrower openings only should be made to push outwards at bottom for ventilation. At f is a piece of halved rough stuff nailed to the front of the post.

The panels, which occupy the lower part of the space between the collar-posts, are filled with pieces of rough plank or " slab," as shown in Fig. 134. These pieces should wear their natural bark as far as possible; they are nailed to the inner boarding.

In Fig. 136 the upper part of a post is in like manner shown in profile : g is the wall-plate in section, and h is the lower end of a rafter. At i will be observed a strip of quartered stuff nailed across the post (with a fir-cone bradded beneath it), which gives a starting-point to the upright k, by which the openwork rustic parapet is supported. These uprights are of small round stuff, slightly flattened on the side towards the post. The openwork parapet is too plainly figured to need description; it is intended to break to a certain extent the straight lines, and partially to conceal the glass-work of the roof, without seriously interfering with sunshine.

So much of the planed wood-work as shows outside should be painted of a good brown, to assimilate with the rustic-work.

CHAPTER XII.

TOOL HOUSES, GARDEN SHELTERS, ETC.

FOR the small rustic tool house shown by Figs. 137 and 138 the materials used are what are known as " slabs " or " rough planks." These are cheap,

Fig. 137.—End Elevation of Rustic Tool House.

and have, when judiciously handled, a good picturesque effect. These slabs are the outside slices cut from logs of rough timber. These slabs generally retain their bark (except in the case of oak), and in most districts they will commonly be of elm. Their thickness and outlines are necessarily irregular : one end will frequently be narrower than the other; and this will account for the arrangement seen in the walls and door of the

Fig. 138.—Side Elevation of Rustic Tool House.

tool house. They are to be bought at saw-mills, and often sold at a fire-wood price. Where their cost is not sensibly increased by carriage, no other material comes so cheaply for building rough sheds. The ordinary country way of using them is as in the horizontal section, Fig. 139. This plan, however, is not suitable for the present

purpose. In so small a structure, rough planks
on the inner side would take up too much space.
It is, therefore, proposed to straighten the edges,
either by sawing or by chopping with the axe, according to circumstances, and lining their inner
sides with thin board. If the cost be not ob-
jected to, ½-in. match-boarding will be neatest
for this purpose; if economy is an object, the
boards of packing-boxes, bought from the grocer,
might suffice. There are, it will be seen, three
sides only to be lined.

Among a lot of rough planks, it is likely that
stuff may be found sufficient for the posts and
other scantling. As to the six pilasters, which
are added for appearance merely, it is possible
that stuff might be found which would, when sawn
to width, do for them; in the illustration they

Fig. 139.—Common Method of Using Slabs.

are supposed to be fir poles or elm saplings;
four sticks only are needed to supply the six
halves and four quarters used.

At the corners are four main posts, 4 in.
square (see a, Fig. 140). These enclose a space
of 7 ft. by 5 ft. (outside measurement). They
are let into the ground 2 ft., and rise 5 ft. 3 in.
above the ground line.

On their tops, and coming flush with their
outer edges, rest the wall-plates, which are 3 in.
deep; these are needed at the back and sides only,
and not at the front. On the same three sides
will also be cross-rails, 2 in. to 3 in. thick, the
ends of which will be let flush into the posts about
a foot from the ground. To the wall-plates and
these rails the slabs are nailed. In the side elevation, Fig. 138, the nails driven into the cross-
rails appear, but not those driven into the wall-

plate, a piece of rough stuff being there shown as fixed over the latter to support the eaves of the thatch.

To the front are to be seen the two door-posts, *b, b,* Fig. 140, which are 2 ft. 8 in. apart, and

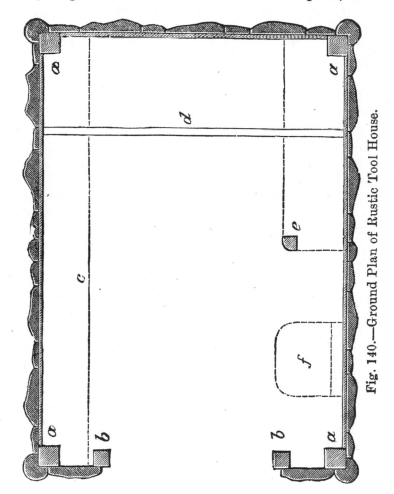

Fig. 140.—Ground Plan of Rustic Tool House.

should be about 3 in. square. As their tops are nailed to the front pair of rafters, they rise to a height of 6 ft. 6 in. The space between door-post and corner-post is filled up by a single slab nailed to the two—5 ft. 6 in. long by 10 in. broad

Above these, instead of a wall-plate, comes the piece of strong slab, shown in Fig. 1 as having an opening cut in it for the head of the door. This is nailed against the door-posts, rafters, etc.

The pilasters are only a matter of ornament. As drawn, they are of halved stuff; the corner ones are so placed that their middles come opposite to the corners of the posts, on the other faces of which pieces of quartered stuff are nailed to meet them. The simple arrangement of the caps of these pilasters, with their decorations of fir cones, is shown on a larger scale in Fig. 141. The horizontal piece beneath the eaves, nailed over the slabs, has the effect of resting on the caps. Beneath the thatch at front and back corresponding pieces are fixed, those at the front being ornamented with fir cones nailed upon them.

The roof is shown in the elevations as thatched. No other covering will look so well, or be so thoroughly in keeping with other parts. The non-professional builder finds it easy to prepare for thatch, any rough stuff serving as rafters and laths, and inequalities being of no account. The rafters for thatch should be arranged about 1 ft., the laths about 6 in. apart.

Should there, however, be reasons for not employing thatch, the building may be more quickly and easily, if not more cheaply, roofed with galvanised iron; only the gables will then best be made sharp instead of blunt, as at present.

Regarding the door, its outer slabs, which appear in Fig. 137, are simply nailed to three ledgers of the same. Being of such rough materials, it will open better if hung on hooks and thimbles than on butt hinges.

The dotted line at c, Fig. 140, marks the projection of a set of shelves, about five in number, which fill the whole of the left-hand side. Of these, the lower will be for flower-pots, the upper for lines, setting-pins, trowels, etc. At d is

shown a strip of wood fixed across the floor to hold
the wheel of the barrow from running back when
that useful vehicle is tilted up against the end
wall, which will be the place assigned for it. In
the gable and upper part of this end will be
hooks or pegs on which to hang the riddle, water-
ing-cans, and such matters. At *e* is an upright

Fig. 141.—Enlarged Cap of Tool House Pilaster.

let into the ground, which, at the height of 2 ft.,
supports rails running to side and back; these
form a kind of stand for spades, forks, and tools
of that description. Above, against the wall·
plate, may be more hooks or pegs.

It is suggested that at *f* a seat might be fixed
to fold down like the leaf of a table when not

wanted. As this building would form a snug
shelter in a shower, such a seat would be a con-
venience; but the more important use of this
space is that slightly below the level of the eaves
it will be fitted with a rack for hoes, rakes, and
similar implements. Such a rack is best made by
boring ½-in. holes in a strip of wood at intervals
of 3 in., and driving pegs into them 5 in. or 6 in.
long. This has to be nailed so that the pegs will
slope upwards, at an angle of about 45°. Rakes,
etc., hung in a rack so made cannot fall.

Figs. 137 and 138 are ⅓ in. to the foot; Fig. 140

Fig. 142.—Garden Snuggery.

is ½ in. to the foot; but Figs. 139 and 141 are not
drawn to scale.

The garden snuggery, of which a general view
is shown at Fig. 142, and a ground plan at Fig
143, is built chiefly of wood, and measures 10 ft
by 7 ft. 8 in. inside, not including the porch,
which is 3 ft. wide; it may serve as a summer-
house. A building as small as this needs but
little foundation. If the ground is level, it is
only necessary to lay four large flat stones on the
surface, A A (Fig. 144), to carry the timbers, the
floor being thus raised enough to keep it dry.

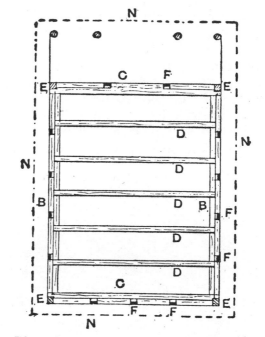

Fig. 143.—Plan of Ground Framework of Garden Snuggery.

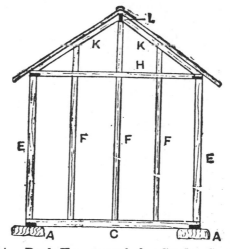

Fig. 144.—Back Framework for Garden Snuggery.

The two side sills B (Fig. 143) are each 10 ft. 8 in.
long, 6 in. wide, and 4 in. thick, and rest on the
stones; on them lie the end sills C C, which are
8 ft. 2 in. long.   These sills are halved together
at the ends, and a hole is bored through them
where the middle of the collar-post will rest. This
hole should be bored a couple of inches into the
stone, and an iron pin or dowel 8 in. long driven
in; the pin will thus stand a couple of inches

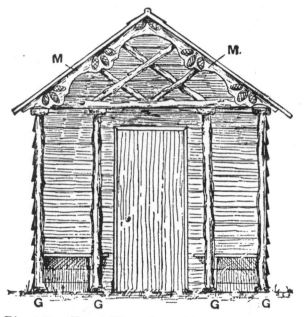

Fig. 145.—Front Elevation of Snuggery Porch.

above the face of the sill, and will fit into a
hole in the collar post.
    The joists D (Fig. 143) for supporting the floor
are five in number, each being 8 ft. long, 2½ in.
wide, and 3 in. deep.   They are halved for a distance of 2 in. at each end to fit into slots, 1½ in.
deep, made for them in the sills, and are nailed
in place.   When fixed their upper surfaces are
level with the sills.
    The four collar-posts E (Figs. 143 and 144) are

each 6 ft. 9 in. long and 4 in. square, and, when set up, their outer sides come flush with the sills. The uprights F (Figs. 143 and 144) are 3 in. square, and need to be 2 in. longer than the collar-posts, as their lower ends are halved for this distance to fit slots in the outer sides of the sills. There are four of each uprights at each side, three at the back and two at the front, the latter serving also as door cheeks. They are nailed in place with their outer sides flush with those of the collar-posts and sills.

For the rustic pillars of the portico G (Fig.

Fig. 146.—Side Elevation of Window-board.

145) nothing will be more suitable than larch poles about 4½ in. in diameter at the base; failing larch, fairly straight pieces of any rough, round wood could be used. The pillars are shown in Figs. 142 and 145 standing upon and dowelled to pieces of stone. When in position, their tops will be level with the collar-posts and uprights, their centres being 2 ft. 4 in. in advance of the front sill.

On the collar-posts, uprights, and pillars are placed the wall plates H (Fig. 144), of which there are four belonging to the snuggery proper, each 5 in. wide and 3 in. thick. The side plates are

13 ft. 4 in. long, and are halved where they rest
on the collar-posts and pillars, to receive the ends
of the cross-plates, which are 8 ft. 2 in. long and
halved to a distance of 5 in. from their ends.
The wall-plates come flush with the collar-posts
and uprights on which they rest, and to which
they are nailed. There is also a fifth wall-plate
which lies along the tops of the pillars in the
front. The best material to use for this would
be half of a pole like those used for the pillars,
the flat side resting on the pillar tops. It will
be observed that the front ends of the side wall-
plates project about 4 in. beyond this piece.

Ten rafters, K (Fig. 144), will be required
for the roof, each 5 ft. long and 3 in. square.
The two outer pairs come flush with the outer
sides of the sills and wall-plates. A sixth pair of
rafters to stand over the pillars and their wall-
plates are made from a round pole cut in half,
with the sawn side laid uppermost. The tops of
the rafters butt against a ridge-piece L (Fig. 144),
made of 1-in. board 4 in. deep and 13 ft. 4 in.
long. As shown in Fig. 144, continuations of the
uprights are in the back carried from the wall-
plate to the roof, the front being treated in a
similar manner.

The lintel of the doorway is 6 ft. above the
sill, the door opening being 5 ft. 11¼ in. by
2 ft. 6 in. after the floor has been laid. The window shown in Fig. 142 is 3 ft. above the sill,
and is 3 ft. high; including the two mullions,
it is 5 ft. 10 in. wide. The board shown nailed
in front of the window sill is sloped a little downwards to throw off the rain, whilst above there is
a board 9 in. wide, nailed at a steeper slope upon
brackets, as seen in Fig. 146, to shelter the window. The ¾-in. flooring boards which are used
for the floor should be bought ready planed on
one side, and must be well seasoned, and cramped
tightly together in laying, or there will be chinks

between them. Similar boards may be used for the outside of the snuggery, being nailed to the uprights at the back and sides, as shown in Fig. 147. At the sides this weather-boarding will extend as far forward as the rustic pillars, thus enclosing the sides of the porch. For the inside of the snuggery use ½-in. matchboarding, as shown in Fig. 147. This may be carried up beneath the rafters to the ridge-piece. The porch may be also matchboarded throughout if desired, although this is not essential.

Fig. 147. Fig. 148.

Figs. 147 and 148.—Sections of Snuggery Walls

There are several methods of making the wooden walls non-conductors of heat, the most thorough being to pack the space between the inner and outer casings with sawdust. Shavings or similar materials could also be used, but less effectually. Another plan is to tack felt over the inner side of the weather-boarding before nailing up the interior casing. But even without any packing, two thicknesses of board with an air space between make a reasonably good non-conductor. Felt is fastened over the matchboard lining of the roof before the iron is put on.

To reduce the cost, the snuggery can be cased

with wood obtained from packing cases. Boards
thus obtained will, of course, be in short lengths,
and will involve more labour; but the design is
so arranged that it will be quite practicable to

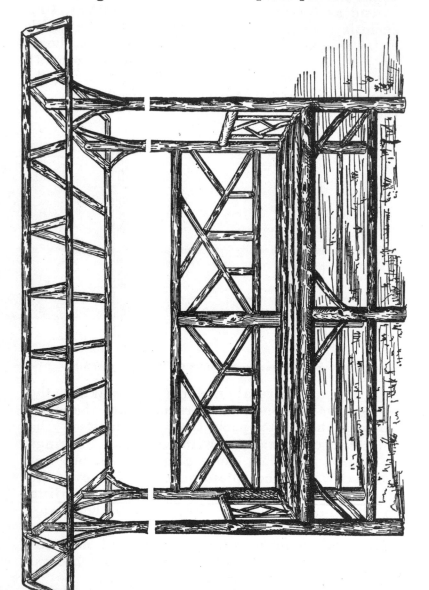

carry it out with them. The short lengths can
be made to fit between the uprights instead of
lying upon them, and the house will thus look as
shown in Fig. 142, the section of the wall being
as shown in Fig. 148, instead of as in Fig. 147.
A strip of lath—that sold for tiling—1 in. wide
and $\frac{5}{8}$ in. thick, is nailed to the sides of the uprights, as shown, and to this the weather-boarding

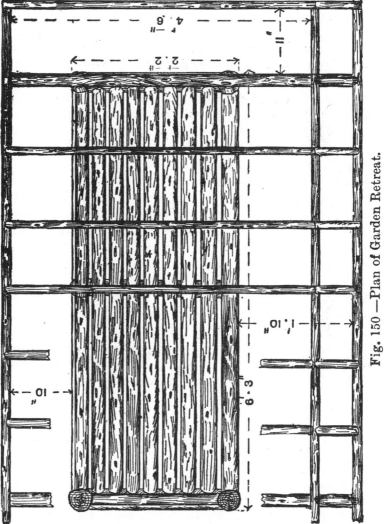

Fig. 150 —Plan of Garden Retreat.

and internal casing are fastened; the effect being
that the walls both inside and out appear to be
divided into long panels.   The effect may be
heightened by painting the framework a darker
colour than the boarding.   In boarding the roof
with this material, the easiest plan will be to nail
the pieces on the upper sides of the rafters, to
cover them with felt, and upon that to screw
the iron.   The space between the two casings of
the walls, although much narrower than before,
can be packed with sawdust, etc.

On reference to Fig. 145 it will be seen that
the caps to the rustic pillars of the porch are
formed by nailing round each pillar four short
pieces of rough wood quartered, the two sawn
sides being placed upwards and inwards.   Four
rough sticks crossing each other fill the space between wall-plate and the rafters.   The bargeboards M M are sawn from $\frac{3}{4}$-in. board, 9 in. wide,
and are nailed to the ends of the side wall-plates
and ridge-piece. They thus project some inches beyond the line of the pillars.   They are shown
ornamented with fir cones bradded on them; virgin cork might be used instead.   The porch may
also have its interior decorated with virgin cork
or with rustic mosaic work.   At each side of the
doorway there is a seat 16 in. high and 14 in.
wide.   The door is made by merely nailing the
boards to four cross-ledgers.

The window lights in Fig. 142 are shown filled
with fancy lead work, which is the most suitable
way of treating them for a building of this kind.
A strip of lath is nailed around the window opening, as in Fig. 148, and the leaded light fastened
in the rebate thus formed with small wire nails,
a little putty being used to make the joints
waterproof.   It will, of course, be much cheaper
to glaze each light with a single sheet of glass
puttied in the rebate, but the effect will not be
so good.   For the roof, fourteen 6 ft. sheets of

corrugated galvanised iron and a 14-ft. run of ridge capping will be needed. The iron should be screwed, not nailed, to the rafters, and should not cost more than 40s., including $1\frac{1}{2}$ gross of galvanised screws and washers. The dotted lines

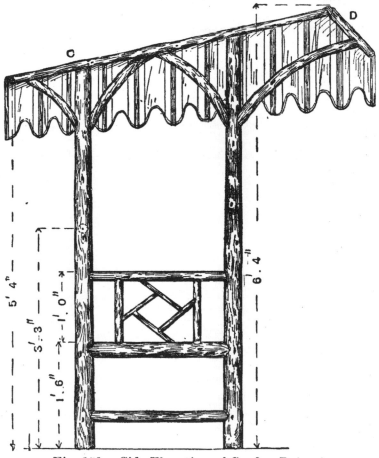

Fig. 151.—Side Elevation of Garden Retreat.

at N N (Fig. 143) indicate the area covered. Its low cost, the ease with which it is fixed, and the few timbers required to carry it, make an iron roof very suitable for a building erected by an amateur workman. It, however, has drawbacks, the chief of which are that it conducts heat too freely, and has not a very artistic appearance. Some precautions against the first defect have already been suggested, and if the snuggery is erected where it will be shaded by trees during the hotter part of the day, this disadvantage will be somewhat overcome. Its inartistic appearance is greatly due to its colour, and some improvement may be made by painting. If surrounded by trees, an iron roof looks very well when painted a reddish-brown colour, while in other situations a buff, or a dull sage green, might be

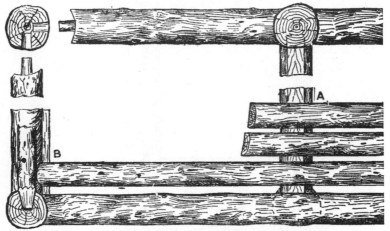

Fig. 152.—Detail of Seat of Garden Retreat.

suitable. The paint needs renewing often. Another method is to cover the roof with trellis work raised a few inches above the iron, and upon this to train ivy or other climbing plants.

It will be better to paint the inside of the snuggery than to paper it, as paper would crack on the boards. Should the second and cheaper plan of boarding be adopted, the rafters, which are left exposed, might be coloured dark brown, and the intermediate spaces of the ceiling painted a buff colour, whilst on the walls a dark sage green might be used for the framework and a lighter sage green for the panels. If the whole interior is lined with matchboarding, according to the first method, the simplest and perhaps best finish would be to use a varnish that had raw or burnt umber ground into it. No fireplace has been provided, but in ordinary winter weather an oil stove would suffice to warm so small a room; if more warmth is wanted, a coal stove might easily be provided, a hole for its pipe being cut through the roof. In either case a ventilator, which can be opened or closed at pleasure, should be arranged near the ridge at each end of the building.

Fig. 153.—Joint of Garden Retreat at c (Fig. 151).

The garden retreat shown in front view by Fig. 149, and in plan and side elevation by Figs. 150 and 151, is constructed from straight unbarked fir saplings, the small twigs of which should be carefully trimmed off. As the bark is to be left on, it should not be cut or bruised; then no artificial finish will be necessary, the bark in itself being sufficient protection against climatic conditions, and presenting the desired rustic appearance. A new feature in the design is the introduction of a roof or canopy, which may be covered with a sun blind as shown in Fig. 151; or a creeping plant may be trained over it.

The two front posts are 3 in. in diameter at

the base by 6 ft. high, and the back posts 3 in. in diameter by 5 ft. 6 in. high; the middle back post is 3 ft. 2 in. high, and the front leg 1 ft. 4 in. The seat rails are $2\frac{1}{2}$ in. in diameter. The front rail is 6 ft. long; the back is in two parts, dowelled to the middle post, which comes between. The side rails are 1 ft. 9 in. long; it is advisable to allow a fair margin for hollowing the ends to fit the posts—3 in. on the length would probably be sufficient. After the ends of the rails have been shaped roughly to fit the posts, they are bored for the reception of $1\frac{1}{8}$-in. oak or elm dowels; these are driven into the rails, and should

Fig 154.—Detail of Front Joints (See c, Fig. 151).

Fig. 155.—Alternative Method of Joining Rails to Posts.

also be a good fit in the posts. The dowel joint is shown in the top corner of Fig. 152.

The lower rungs, arm-rests, and back rails are jointed to the posts by tapering their ends slightly, and then tapering the dowel holes to suit with a gouge, so that the rails will just drive up nicely; this joint is shown in the bottom corner of Fig. 152. The rails, etc., are finally driven home, and secured with nails or screws inserted at suitable angles. The back and the side panels are filled with twigs about $1\frac{1}{4}$ in. in diameter, the ends of the twigs being trimmed to fit the rails, and afterwards nailed in position.

The seat battens are half-round in section, and are cut from 3-in. saplings, the flat part being placed downwards. The method of fixing them is shown in Figs. 152, 156, and 157. The seat having been fitted, the struts under the seat rails are next cut and fixed in position.

The canopy must now be put together. The tops of the posts are first hollowed to form a seating for 2¼-in. saplings, 4 ft. 6 in. long; these act as principal rafters. Before nailing or screwing them to the posts, it is advisable to sight across them to see if they are in the same plane; any alteration that may be required to bring them to lie in the same angle can be effected at the seating on the top of the posts. The halved joint at each end of the principals should also be cut

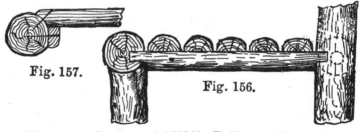

Fig. 157.

Fig. 156.

Fig. 156.—Section of Middle Rail at A (Fig. 152).
Fig 157.—Detail of Middle Rail at B (Fig. 152).

(before fixing up) for receiving the purlins; the principals are further steadied with struts screwed or nailed to the posts. The purlins are about 2 in. in diameter by 8 ft. 6 in. long, and are fixed to the halved joint previously made on the principal rafters. Smaller twigs, which act as common rafters, are in turn fixed to the purlins. Fig. 153 shows the method of jointing at the back of the canopy at c (Fig. 151), and Fig. 154 is the detail of the front joints. Fig. 129 (p. 94) is the top of the post hollowed to receive the principal rafter, Fig. 155 is an alternative method of joining the rails to the posts, Fig. 156 is a section near the middle rail at A (Fig. 152), while Fig. 157 is a detail of middle rail at B (Fig. 152).

CHAPTER XIII.

SUMMER-HOUSES.

THE lean-to summer-house shown by Fig. 158 is intended for a small garden. Perhaps in no better way can a dead wall or the back of some

Fig. 158.—Lean-to Summer-house.

unsightly outhouse be better utilised than as the background for such a building. The dimensions of the structure are: length, 8 ft.; breadth, 3 ft. 3 in.; height, 8 ft.

Its general arrangement is seen in the ground plan (Fig. 159). Four pillars, A, B, B, A, occupy the front. These are poles 3½ in. or 4 in. in diameter. Any rough and tolerably straight wood will do, but larch is to be preferred. These rise

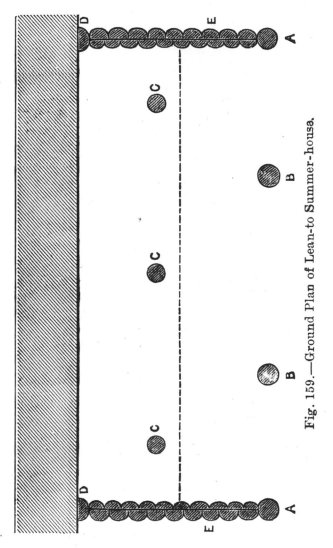

Fig. 159.—Ground Plan of Lean-to Summer-house.

5 ft. above ground, and should not have less than 2 ft. below the surface. The dwarf pillars c supporting the seat are of similar stuff, but rather smaller. They show 14 in. above, and

should be buried about 9 in. below ground.   The
pilasters D are of rather larger stuff sawn in half.
These are only 5 ft. long, as they need not enter

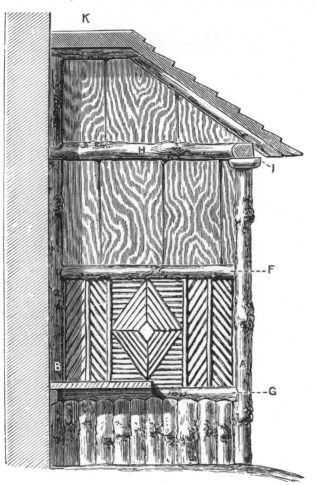

Fig. 160.—Elevation of Inside of End of Lean-to
Summer-house.

into the ground, being fixed only by strong nails
to the wall.

The ends of the summer-house (the space
from A to D) are of smaller half-stuff, ranged
side by side (as seen at E, E), and nailed to the

cross-pieces, F and G, which appear in Fig. 160.
In this last-named figure also appears one of the
wall-plates, resting on and nailed to the tops
of the pillars (H, at Fig. 160), and at I is seen
where one of the front wall-plates meets it. There
are two of these front wall-plates, each resting on
the two pillars to right and left of the entrance,
and their inner ends appear in Fig. 158, where the
ends of the purlins which form the small gable
rest upon them. The wall-plates are of large
half-stuff, with the flat side above. In Fig. 160
will be seen how the short cross-piece which carries
the sloping end of the roof is supported; and
Fig. 161, which is a section through the centre of
the building, explains how the ridge-piece of the
small gable, E, rests at its inner end on a cross-
piece M from rafter to rafter, seen in section
only, whilst N shows the point at which the purlins meet and support the ridge-piece towards its
outer end. The intersection of the diagonal
braces in the gable is indicated at O, and P shows
the course of one of the rafters, and how its
upper end rests against the wall, and upon a
ridge-piece of half-stuff, Q, strongly nailed to the
masonry.

The elevation (Fig. 158) explains pretty clearly
the ornamental details of the front. They are
not elaborate. It will be seen that the top of
each pillar has a small cap, formed of four pieces
of quartered stuff, mitred at the corners, and
that across the opening on each side of the entrance, near the top, is a " transom " of straight
wood, with a little arrangement of crooked bangles round it. Over the entrance are diagonal
braces crossing, and also a little filling-in with
bangles. The entrance is 5 ft. 10 in. high.

In order that an ornamental and appropriate
lining may be given to the back of our summer-
house, it is recommended to plug the wall, and
nail over it a level covering of thin boards—

say, ½-in. matchboarding. Upon this the decorative work can be bradded. The back of the seat
is shown in Fig. 158 to be of rustic mosaic. Above
this, as well as under the seats, a covering of bark
has been introduced. British-grown bark, such
as elm, can be made to lie flat, but as in any
but rural.districts this may be difficult to get,
virgin cork may be made to take its place.

Fig. 160 gives an inside view of one of the
ends, and from this it will be seen that the ornamentation of those parts varies little from that
of the back. The lower band, however, answering
to the strip under the seats, is not bark, which, in
this place, would be liable to be kicked and de-
stroyed by the feet, but of smaller half-stuff, so
arranged as to break joint with the outside pieces.
This will be seen by referring to the ground plan.
Any chinks in the ends should be neatly tucked
with moss, so as to make them wind-proof.

The roof is of wooden shingles—things which
any rough hand at carpentry can prepare and
put on for himself. As will be seen from Fig. 158,
it is easy to give an ornamental character to
these. They will have a rustic look, which will
go well with other parts of the structure, and, if
clumsily made, the effect will be none the worse.
For the present purpose, suppose the shingles to
be 12 in. by 4 in. The lower ends may be sawn
to a variety of ornamental shapes.

If this covering is used, instead of nailing
laths across the rafters, it is proposed to cover
the whole roof with similar boarding to the back,
and upon this it is a simple thing to nail the shingles, placing them just as tiles might be placed.
Whilst nailing them on, it will be necessary to
have some person within to hold a heavy hammer
against the place, otherwise the vibration will jar
off the shingles as fast as they are fixed. A ¾-in.
board, rather wider than half the length of the
shingles, should first be nailed along the eaves.

to make up the required thickness. It will be noticed that the ends of the rafters are made to project so as to give a good breadth of eaves—a

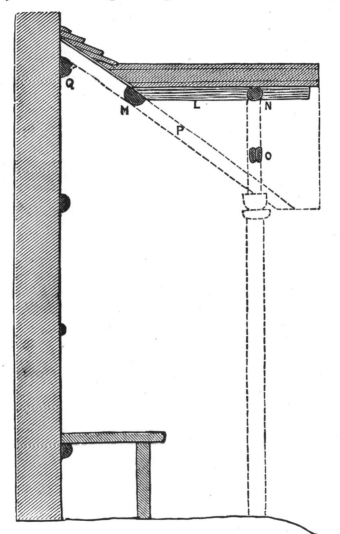

Fig 161.—Section through Centre of Lean-to Summer-house.

desirable feature in so narrow a building, alike for shade, shelter, and the appearance of cosiness. If, however, the roof should be thatched, the projecting rafters will be unnecessary, as the thatch alone will form sufficient eaves.

Down the "valleys" at the juncture of the main roof and the entrance gable a strip of zinc will, of course, be nailed before the shingles are put on, whilst along the ridges a strip of zinc will be nailed upon the shingles; and this latter will need painting to match the colour of the wood.

Various suggestions may be given for finishing the inside of the roof. Supposing that round or half-round larch stuff has been used for the rafters (the latter is to be preferred for shingles, as giving a level surface to board upon), the space between the rafters may be covered with bark— virgin cork or otherwise—the chinks being stuffed with moss. But if this is done it will be well to fix the bark with screws, as the vibration caused by driving nails would displace or loosen the shingles.

A second plan under the like circumstances would be before nailing the boards upon the rafters to stretch matting across the latter—either ordinary garden bast matting or, better, the more substantial rush matting, both of which are very inexpensive. These have a pleasant natural colour (the last-named especially, of a greenish hue), and are so unartificial in their structure as to appear in no way out of place among rustic work.

Or it may so happen that suitable larch stuff is not to hand, and that ordinary sawn scantling has to be used for the rafters. If so, the whole roof may be hung with ling; or the rush matting may be stretched across the lower side of the rafters and tacked there, being afterwards more completely secured and finished by nailing a split hazel or other rod down the middle of each rafter. This last plan makes a neat and pleasing roof.

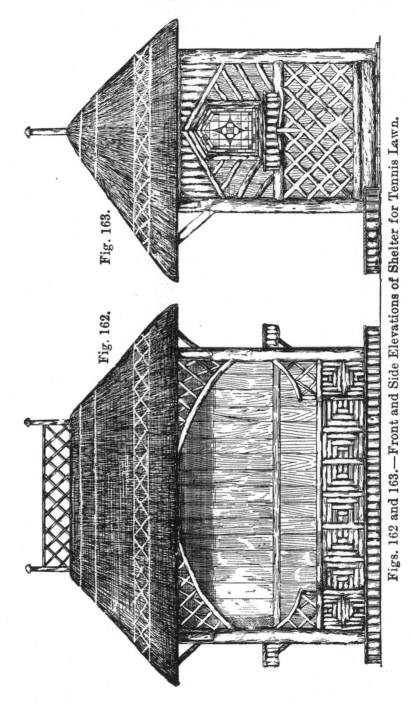

Fig. 163.

Fig. 162.

Figs. 162 and 163.—Front and Side Elevations of Shelter for Tennis Lawn.

It scarcely needs to be said that to make such a summer-house look its best the wall on each side ought to be covered with ivy or other creepers; and it will also be obvious that, if the height of the wall permits the floor of the summer-house to be raised a step or two above the sur-

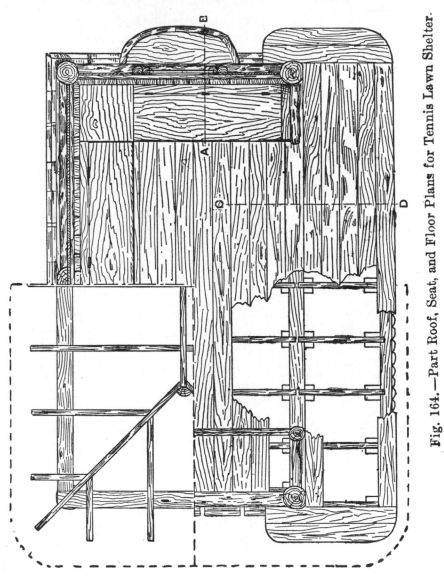

Fig. 164.—Part Roof, Seat, and Floor Plans for Tennis Lawn Shelter.

rounding level, the structure will gain thereby both in effectiveness of appearance and in pleasantness as a place in which to sit.

The rustic summer-house or tennis lawn shelter illustrated in front and side elevations by Figs.

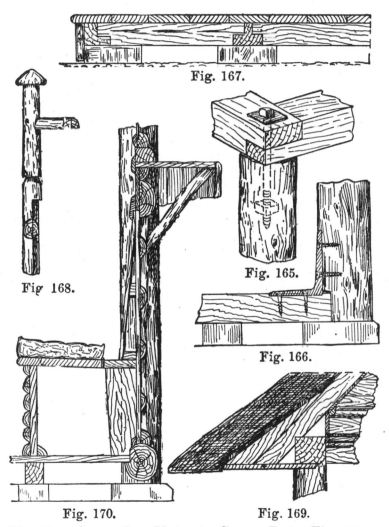

Fig. 167.

Fig. 168.

Fig. 165.

Fig. 166.

Fig. 170.   Fig. 169.

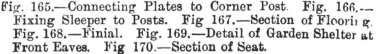

Fig. 165.—Connecting Plates to Corner Post. Fig. 166.— Fixing Sleeper to Posts. Fig 167.—Section of Flooring. Fig. 168.—Finial. Fig. 169.—Detail of Garden Shelter at Front Eaves. Fig 170.—Section of Seat.

162 and 163 is constructed from straight saplings and twigs that have had their bark removed, and have been subjected to a reasonable period of seasoning. A new feature in the design is the accommodation under the seats for the reception of the croquet or tennis gear, and also the extended eaves and floor (see Fig. 164) and the open front, giving at once an uninterrupted view of the game and shelter from the direct rays of the sun.

The shelter is 10 ft. long by 5 ft. 6 in. wide, the height from the floor to the eaves being 6 ft. 3 in., and from the floor to the ridge 9 ft. The four posts are 6 ft. 9 in. long by 6 in. in diameter. The middle and lower end and the back rails are tenoned to the posts, a flat being formed on the post by the mortise and a corresponding shoulder on the rails. The remaining portion is worked to fit roughly the contour of the post.

The plates are 5 in. by 5 in. in section, and are secured to the posts with long galvanised bolts and nuts and a 3½-in. square washer under the heads of the bolts. When halving the front plate, allow it to house into the side plates 1½ in.; by this method it will have a bearing on both posts. In Fig. 165 the left-hand plate represents the front. The front posts are connected at the floor line by a scantling, 4 in. by 3 in., which also forms a sleeper for the floor joists; see Figs. 166 and 167.

The structure rests on a low plinth of bricks, spaces being left for the circulation of air under the floor.

The extended floor also rests on bricks placed immediately below the joists; see Fig. 167, which is a section on C D (Fig. 164). The twig plinth nailed around the front will effectually conceal the sleeper and brick foundation.

The rafters are 2½ in. by 3 in., and the ridge and hip rafters 2 in. by 5 in., the finials (see

Fig. 168) being nailed between the angles of tne hips. The eaves in front project 2 ft. beyond the posts, and Fig. 169 shows the method by which the additional width is obtained.

The sides are filled with $\frac{5}{8}$-in. vee-grooved and

Fig. 171.—Strapping Cushion to Seat.

Fig. 172.—Front Elevation of Octagonal Summer-house.

tongued boarding, to which is attached the rustic work.

The stained glass windows are fixed, and on the outer side of the back are diagonal braces made from split saplings, while in the centre a vertical post runs from sill to plate.

The braces and post are shown in the plan (Fig. 164).

The seats are constructed to form lockers (see Fig. 170, which is a section at A B, Fig. 164), their height being 1 ft. 3 in., which, with the addition of a 3-in. cushion, will form comfortable sitting accommodation.

The cushions are retained in place by straps passing through slots and fastening over suitable studs on the under side; see Fig. 171. This method provides a means of easily removing and quickly replacing the cushions when required for use. A space of 3 in., or a distance equal to the thickness of the cushions, must be left at the sloping back, to allow the seat to open properly.

The nature of the locker is partly concealed by the rustic work of split twigs that is nailed to the front.

Next fix the lattice work between the finials and under the front plate. The short struts on the front posts are more for effect than for any real support.

The roof is boarded on the inside, the work being carried on the rafters as far as the collar ties, and continued flat on these. Moulding is fixed in the angles formed between the rafters and ties, and a cornice is fixed at the plates. The heels of the rafters and plates are also boarded around, as shown in Fig. 169.

The roof may be covered with thatch of wheat, straw, reeds, broom, or heather, and the whole of the woodwork visible should be varnished.

The summer-house illustrated by Fig. 172 is suited to a garden of moderate size, one in which space is not so restricted as to necessitate crowding the building close against a wall. This octagonal summer-house has a continuous seat some 15 ft. long. From side to side each way it measures 10 ft. Fig. 172 is an elevation of the front of the house.

Its framework and the main part of it are of larch poles; other woods are, however, used for

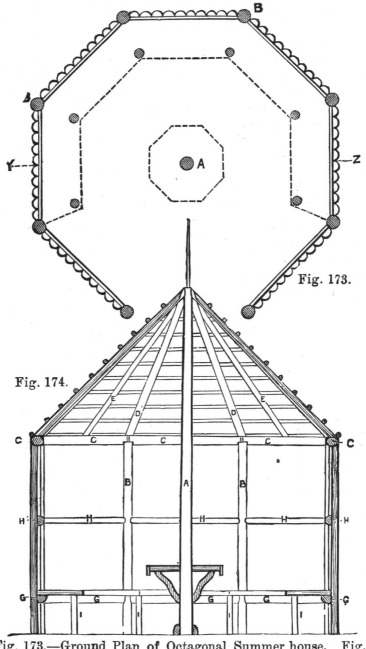

Fig. 173.

Fig. 174.

Fig. 173.—Ground Plan of Octagonal Summer house. Fig. 174.—Section of Octagonal Summer-house at Y Z (Fig. 173), showing Framework.

minor purposes. The roof is of thatch. In the
arrangement of this building there is a certain
resemblance to a tent. It has a central pillar, A,
not unlike a tent pole, which sustains much of
the weight of the roof. Being of first importance,
this pillar is somewhat larger than any of the
other timbers—say 6 in. in diameter near its
bottom, and tapering as little as may be. A
rod of iron or wood rises from its top to form
the centre of the straw pinnacle seen crowning the
roof in Fig. 172. This pillar shows a height of
11 ft. 2 in. above ground, and it should be let
3 ft. or more into the soil; for it will need to be
firmly fixed, or it may be forced out of the per-
pendicular during the erection of the roof; when
the roof timbers are once fixed in place, it will
have little further chance of moving. The dia-
gram Fig. 173 is a ground plan, and Fig. 174
is a section showing the timbers from the interior; both are drawn on a scale of ¼ in. to the
foot.

The eight collar-posts (B, Figs. 173 and 174) at
the corners of the octagon are of somewhat smaller
stuff—say 4 in. They show 6 ft. above ground,
and should have 2 ft. below. It will be well to
gas-tar all the underground work.

The ground plan of a building in this shape
is readily laid out. The space being levelled, a
string is taken which has a loop at each end,
and is 5 ft. 2 in. long. With a stake driven
through the loop at one end as a centre, and with
a stick passed through the loop at the other to
serve as the travelling leg of the compasses, a
circle is struck 10 ft. 4 in. in diameter, and into
this pegs are driven at equal intervals (4 ft.
apart) to mark the centres of the eight collar-
posts. Whilst digging the holes for the posts,
these points are kept by drawing two straight
lines on the ground which intersect at the peg.

The cross-pieces which rest on the collar-posts,

and which serve as wall-plates, are a trifle smaller stuff than the posts—say 3 in. Fig. 175 shows how they are cut to fit the tops of the posts, and nailed there. In this building there are no mortise and tenon joints. On these ends above the posts rest the lower ends of the eight main rafters, D, the upper ends of which rest against and are nailed to the central pillar. The eight intermediate rafters, E, rest at the bottom on the middles of the side plates, and at top are cut to fit upon and between the tops of the main rafters.

Fig. 175.—Collar Posts and Ends of Wall Plates.

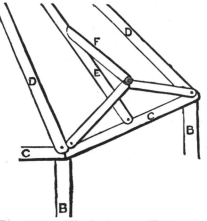

Fig. 176.—Timbers over Entrance of Octagonal Summer-house.

The laths used are in this case in no way particular—any sticks will do; they will not be seen, and under thatch there is no necessity that a level surface should be formed by them, as for slates or tiles. They are nailed 6 in. or 8 in. apart.

The gable over the entrance is arranged as in Fig. 176. The laths, when nailed on, will have to run over the little ridge formed by F, instead of keeping the level, as on the other sides. This will cause no special difficulties in the thatching.

The walls are of larch poles sawn in half. To split a number of heavy poles with the hand saw is tedious work, and it is better to get them run through by the nearest steam saw. The quantity of half-stuff required may be easily calculated; one of these sides will take about five and a half 6-ft. lengths of 4-in. stuff. The tops of these wall-pieces are sawn obliquely to fit against the round wall-plates to which they are nailed. In their lower parts they are nailed to the lower cross-pieces, G, G, G, Fig. 174.

These latter will best be made of rather large stuff quartered, since their upper sides on which the seat-boards rest should be level, as well as their backs, which go against the wall-pieces. The middle cross-pieces are of smaller half-stuff, and should be nailed to the wall-pieces rather than that the wall-pieces should be nailed to them; for they are in a conspicuous place, and nails driven through them and clenched would be unsightly.

The front supports of the seats are let into the ground some 6 in., and rise 14½ in. above the ground line. The seats should be cut from 1-in. board, and should be about 16½ in. wide.

In the two window sides of the octagon (see Figs. 177 and 172), the space below the windows is filled with whole poles, their bottoms resting on a sill let in level with the ground, and their tops nailed into through a cross-piece of half-stuff (K, Fig. 177). The mullions and transoms of the windows—mere sticks—are of small straight larch stuff, but the ornamental filling in above is of crooked branches—oak bangles by preference, though apple-wood would do very well. It often happens that an old apple-tree is cut down, and at once condemned as firewood; yet its stem may have grotesque knots, and its branches picturesque contortions which would make it valuable for rustic work. Whenever rustic building is contemplated, it is well that such wood should be laid by; a single tree would supply all the small quantity of crooked stuff that is required in the present instance. Even the interlaced stems of ivy, when an old growth has covered a wall, have sometimes been utilised to excellent effect.

It may be observed that any chinks between the pieces beneath the windows, as well as in

Fig. 177.—Window Side of Octagonal Summer-house.

the walls generally, are most readily and appro-priately rendered wind-proof by neatly stuffing with moss. Fig. 177 gives a full front elevation of one of the window sides (they being only seen obliquely in Fig. 172), and it is on the $\frac{1}{2}$-in. scale.

Four stout crooked pieces are used as struts to support the table (drawn to 1 in. scale in Figs.

178 and 179); ¾-in. board will suffice for the top
of this table, and it will probably be cut from
two widths. To give proper strength to the ornamental border (seen in Fig. 179), a second thickness of the board is attached below each corner,
extending 3 or 4 in. to each side, so as to allow
each of the longer bits of split rod to be fixed,
as shown, with two brads.

A really satisfactory material in which to
finish the top of a rustic table is not easily found;
it must give a level surface, and at the same time
be in harmony with its surroundings. Board,
planed or painted, oilcloth, or any manufactured
material, is felt to be out of place; marble or
slate looks cold and hard. Nothing that is abso-
lutely level satisfies the requirements; the best
alternative is rustic mosaic. By this is meant
split rods of wood so bradded down as to form
patterns. For the present purpose, however, the
mosaic must be kept more neat and smooth than
usual. Fig. 178 shows the top of the table thus
treated.

The rods most in favour for rustic mosaic
are those of the hazel. They are to be bought
cheaply and abundantly when the undergrowth of
woods is cut. They have a smooth and pretty
bark, and the useful size is from ¾ in. to 1½ in.
Sticks of other kinds of the same size can also
be used : birch and wild cherry may be named
among those with smooth bark, and wych elm and
maple among those with rough; willow or withy,
again, is of most common growth, and exceedingly
useful. In river-side neighbourhoods it is often
the cheapest and most plentiful of all woods.
For mosaic work, it is always peeled, for its bark
is unattractive, and its light colour when stripped
makes it tell well in contrast to the dark bark
of other woods. If used, as it often is, for out-
door purposes in garden carpentry, it should
always be peeled. Country carpenters have a

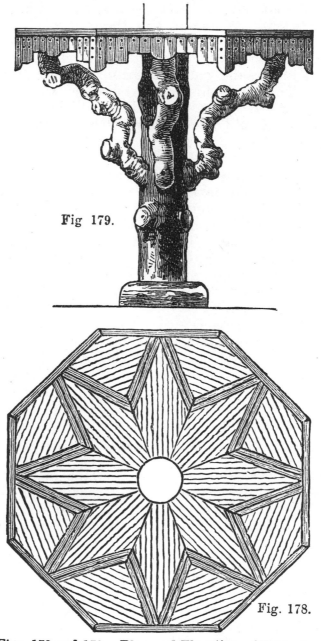

Fig 179.

Fig. 178.

Figs. 178 and 179.—Plan and Elevation of Table for
Octagonal Summer-house.

saying that withy lasts twice as long without its
bark as with it; and in this there is much truth,
for the loose bark holds the wet to the wood and
causes it to rot. To make it peel freely, it should
be cut just as the young leaves make their appearance. The like holds good with other woods; but
if it is desired that the bark should hold firmly,
the wood should be cut down in dead of winter,
when all the sap is down.

The top of the table is supposed to be mainly
composed of peeled withy. The pattern contains
only the double dark line bounding the star and
the single strip round the edge in hazel. So much
white will not look amiss in this place, and withy
is easily worked. Hazel and most woods twist
so much in the grain that it is rarely safe to
split them except with the saw, but withy—in
short lengths like these, at least—can be split with
a hatchet.

In rough carpentry there is no more pretty or
interesting work than these mosaics. The backs
of the seats (Fig. 180), and the seats themselves
(Fig. 181), are decorated in this way. On the
seats themselves, as on the table top, hazel and
withy are contrasted, and form a design in alter-
nate triangles; the separating bands, it may be
noticed, have a light strip against the dark, and
a dark strip against the light, triangle. Along the
edge of the seats one or two strips merely are
nailed lengthwise. In such a situation an ornamental edging like that round the table would
be too liable to be broken. It is recommended
that the back of the seats should be in dark bark-
covered woods only, for the mosaic in that position
will look better without any mixture of the light-
coloured withy.

The upper compartments of the sides with
which the backs of those sitting down will not
come in contact may be more quickly and yet
pleasingly covered with sheets of bark. Elm bark

is good for the purpose. It may be peeled in large
sheets from the trunks of trees felled in spring,
when the sap is rising; and whilst it is drying
should have bricks or stones laid on it to press
it flat. When dried, it is nailed to the walls, and
any cracks which appear can be neatly filled with

Fig. 180.—Seat Side of Octagonal Summer-house.

moss. The space beneath the seats is also shown
as roughly covered with bark.

The almost conical roof is thatched. No other
covering is so pleasing as thatch for a rustic building. Its colour and rough texture harmonise well
with the natural wood, and all its associations
are of a rustic character; no other covering so
effectually excludes the summer heat, and no-

where can one find a retreat so suggestive of cool-
ness, quiet, and repose, as under the low eaves
of a thatched building. Thatch has, it must be
admitted, certain practical disadvantages—birds
and winds are apt to scatter fragments from it,
and it needs renewing at comparatively short intervals. The common saying is that a thatched
roof needs re-coating every ten years. Often,
no doubt, this is near the truth, yet really good
work will frequently stand for almost twenty
years. The materials in use in this country are
reeds, straw, and stubble. Reeds make a strong
thatch, but are not easily to be procured, except
in fenny districts. Stubble, which is the lower
and stronger part of the wheat stem, stands
better than straw, which is its upper and weaker
portion; to last properly, however, stubble should
be cut immediately after harvest, and should not
be left standing, as it frequently is, till the
spring, for then the winter rains, collecting in
its hollow stems, cause it to rot before it is cut.
On small buildings like summer-houses especially,
stubble makes a much more compact and sightly
roof than straw.

Thatching is not costly or difficult work. In
agricultural districts a load of stubble—sufficient
to thatch three such buildings as the one illustrated—costs 30s., and a thatcher expects the
wages of a first-class labourer only, not those
of a mechanic. He needs an assistant, whose busi-
ness it is to straighten the material into convenient bundles (called "yelvens"), and to supply
him as he requires them. If he is re-thatching an
old building, he merely thrusts the ends of his
new material into the old thatch with a wooden
spud; but if he is covering a new roof he sews
down his "yelvens" to the laths and rafters with
a huge needle and stout tarred string. He begins
at the eaves, laying as wide a breadth as he can
conveniently reach on one side of his ladder, this

breadth being called a "stelch." He works upwards, each new layer covering the tar-cord which
secures that beneath it; and thus he goes on till
he has reached the ridge.

In his second "stelch" he is careful to blend
together its edge and the edge of that already
laid, so that no rain may find its way between
them; and in doing this completely lies much of
the superiority of good over bad thatching. When
laid, the thatch is smoothed down and straightened with a gigantic comb, like the head of a
large rake, one end being without teeth, and
serving as a handle. In the present instance,
the tops of all the stelches meeting in a point are

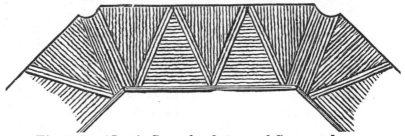

Fig. 181.—Mosaic Seats for Octagonal Summer-house.

finished and capped by the little bundle of thatching material forming the pinnacle, which is
tightly bound round the rod of wood or iron in
its centre.

It is usual to bind thatching down with at least
two belts of buckles and runners. In the summer-
house (Fig. 172) two double belts are shown. The
buckles have some resemblance to ladies' hair-
pins on a colossal scale. They are made of slips
of withy, twisted and doubled in their middles
and pointed at their ends; the runners are long
straight slips of the same. These latter are laid
across the thatch, and the buckles, being placed
over them, are pushed tightly into it—their points
being driven upwards, that wet may not be let

into the roof by them. The short diagonal runners seen in the illustration crossing each other
between the horizontal lines are used in ornamental thatching only, and are rather for appearance than for use. Lastly, the eaves are cut to
shape, and trimmed with paring-knife and shears.

The roof looks most pretty and cosy within if
lined with ling. The ling is fixed in a way somewhat akin to thatching. A layer is placed along
the bottom opposite to the eaves, and secured by a
strip of wood nailed from rafter to rafter; the
layer next above hides this strip, and so the work
is carried on to the apex, where a knot cut from
an apple-tree trunk, a bunch of fir-cones fastened
together, or some such matter, finishes the whole.
In districts where ling is not to be had, gorse
or furze in short pieces may serve instead, but
stout gloves are required to handle it; or the ends
of fir branches may do, if nothing better offers.

It is not always easy to decide on the best
way of forming a floor. Boards may look out of
place. A pitching of pebbles is more in character :
it is dry and cleanly, and especially if some
variety of colour is obtainable, and the stones are
arranged in some geometrical design, it may add
to the ornamental effect. Pebbles are not, however, pleasing to the feet of those who wear thin
shoes. Gravel, where it is always dry, is apt to
become dusty, and to disagree with ladies' dresses.
If, however, gravel should be used, perhaps the
best plan to prevent the rising of damp, and to
obviate dust as far as possible, is to asphalt it :
on the foundation of broken stones and a layer
of coarse gravel to put a course of asphalt or of
ordinary gas tar, and on this to sift enough fine
washed gravel to hide it. Yet a wood pavement
of small larch poles, cut into 5- or 6-in. billets,
and pitched with some attention to geometrical
arrangement, will make the most dry and comfortable of floors, and one which will not harmonise

badly with any of the decorative work of our summer-house.

The octagonal house illustrated by Fig. 182 is made up of varnished rustic work. The saplings and twigs should be as straight and as regular as possible, and divested of their bark.

Fig 182.—Octagonal Summer-house with Three Gables.

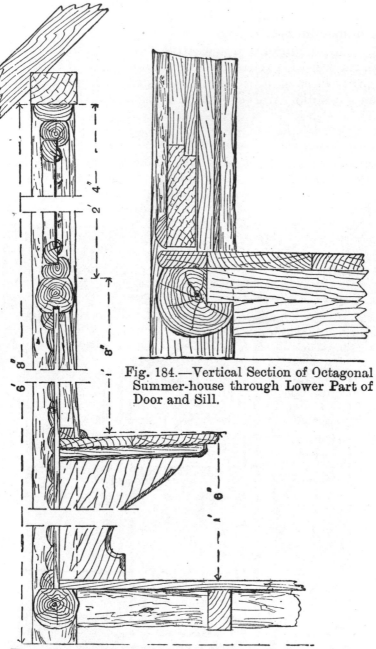

Fig. 184.—Vertical Section of Octagonal
Summer-house through Lower Part of
Door and Sill.

Fig. 183.—Vertical Section of Octagonal Summer-house
through Side Casement.

The eight posts are 4 in. in diameter by
6 ft. 8 in. long. The short sill pieces are also
4 in. in diameter, while the middle rails are 3½ in.
in diameter, and the plate is 3 in. by 4½ in. The

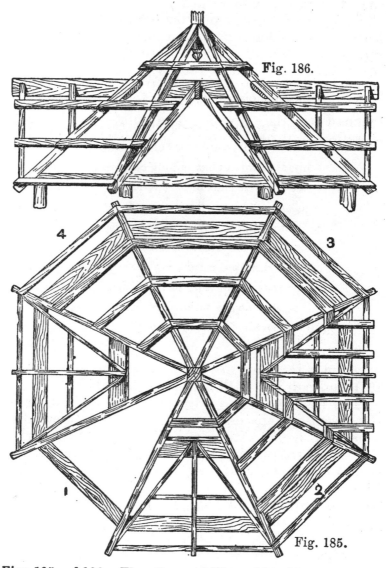

Fig. 186.

4

3

1

2

Fig. 185.

Figs. 185 and 186.—Elevation and Plan of Roof for Octagonal
Summer-house.

floor and roof are constructed from ordinary scantlings.

The posts form a circle 6 ft. 6 in. in diameter. They are spaced about 2 ft. 3 in. apart, except the door-posts, which are 2 ft. 7 in. centres. Flats may be worked on the posts for the better fitting of the door, panels, and casements, and the top edge of the sill is also planed flat to receive the floorboards, and a rebate is formed for the $\frac{5}{8}$-in. matchboard (see Fig. 183).

The sill and middle rails are scribed and stub-tenoned to the posts. The plate is halved, dowelled, and nailed to the posts. The joists are

Fig. 187.—Securing Glass to Rustic Casement

2 in. by 4 in., and are notched to the sills (Fig. 184) and covered with 1-in. floorboards.

The roof is formed with three gables, four being deemed unnecessary, as a summer-house is generally fixed with its back to a shrubbery. Eight hip rafters are required, and by fixing the heels of each pair of rafters on the sides of the plate marked 1, 2, 3, and 4 (see Fig. 185) more space is acquired for the gables. The ridges and valley-pieces of the gables are attached to a wide batten screwed to the under side of the hip rafters (see Figs. 185 and 186). Some of the small battens are omitted from Fig. 185 to give a better view of the gables, etc.

The roof-covering is generally wheat straw, with a top dressing of either broom or heather. The dark colour of the two latter materials har-

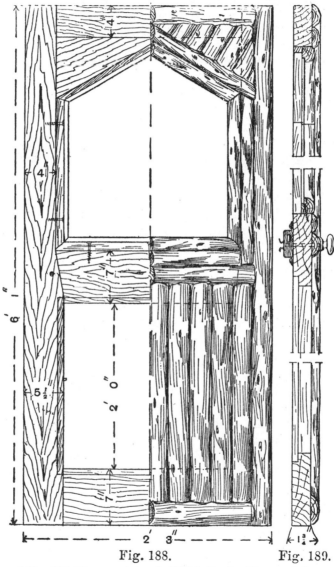

Fig. 188. Fig. 189.

Fig. 188.—Half Front and Half Back View of Door for Octagonal Summer-house. Fig. 189.—Section of Door for Octagonal Summer-house.

monises much better with a varnished house than
does a covering wholly of straw. The four lower
panels are filled in with matchboarding, which is
carried right up to the plate in the three back
divisions. The rustic work, excepting the back
panels, is then fitted and nailed.

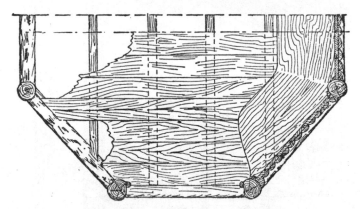

Fig. 190.—Part Plan of Octagonal Summer-house.

There are four casement windows, which open
outward. A section of casement and frame enlarged is shown in Fig. 187. A shallow rebate
is formed to receive the leaded lights, which are
retained in position with split bamboo fixed with
round-headed brass screws.

The door (Figs. 188 and 189) is 6 ft. 1 in. by
2 ft. 3 in. The rustic work is overlaid on the
frame of the door. The centre of the diamond-
shaped panel is filled with cork. The top panel

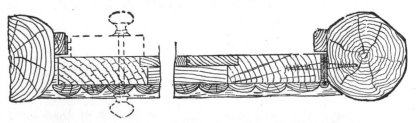

Fig. 191.—Horizontal Section through Door Posts.

is glazed with stained glass. Three butts and a rim lock are fitted on the inside of the door, and the lower panel is filled with matchboarding.

Some further illustrations may be noted. Fig. 190 is a part plan of the octagonal summer-house;

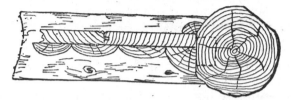

Fig. 192.—Part Section of Side Panel.

Fig. 191, horizontal section through door-posts; Fig. 192, part section of a side panel; Fig. 193, method of fixing plate to posts; and Fig. 194, finial.

A seat 13 in. wide, supported on wide battens, which in turn rest on shaped brackets, is fixed at each angle. A sloping back (see Fig. 183) is

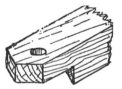

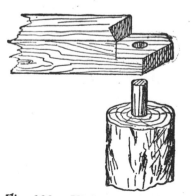

Fig. 193.—Fixing Plate to Posts.

Fig. 194.—Finial.

fitted, which adds to the general comfort. The decoration of the inside should now receive attention. The floor may be covered with linoleum, the seats carpeted or cushioned. The sloping backs of the seats and the walls will look well if covered with Indian matting or Japanese leather paper. Split cane or bamboo may be used with good effect at the joints or angles. The under side of the roof or ceiling should be first covered by stretching canvas across the rafters, and to this is attached the decorative material.

The summer-house stands on stone slabs raised about 1 in. above the ground. The lower ends of the posts are dressed with pitch, or are stood on sheet lead. The triangular spaces in the gables can be made to open inwards if desired, and used for ventilation.

INDEX